Richard S. Andrews

Andrews' Mounted Artillery Drill

Compiled according to the latest regulations from standard military authority

Richard S. Andrews

Andrews' Mounted Artillery Drill
Compiled according to the latest regulations from standard military authority

ISBN/EAN: 9783337317379

Printed in Europe, USA, Canada, Australia, Japan

Cover: Foto ©ninafisch / pixelio.de

More available books at **www.hansebooks.com**

ANDREWS'
MOUNTED ARTILLERY DRILL;

COMPILED

ACCORDING TO THE LATEST REGULATIONS

FROM

STANDARD MILITARY AUTHORITY,

BY

R. SNOWDEN ANDREWS.

LIEUTENANT-COLONEL COMMANDING BATTALION ARTILLERY.

CHARLESTON:
EVANS AND COGSWELL.
1863.

Entered, according to Act of Congress, in the year 1863, by
R. SNOWDEN ANDREWS,
In the Clerk's Office of the District Court of the Confederate States for the District of Charleston, South Carolina.

By permission, this work is dedicated to "The Christian Soldier," Lieutenant-General T. J. JACKSON, by his late Chief of Division Artillery, as a slight token of appreciation of the kindness of the following complimentary language: "For Major Andrews' gallant and meritorious conduct in the Battle of Cedar Run, I respectfully recommend that his appointment date from that battle."

However worthless this work in itself may be, it assumes something of value in the author's eyes when thus rendered a tribute of respect to "Old Stonewall."

R. SNOWDEN ANDREWS,
Lieutenant-Colonel Commanding Battalion Artillery.

Milford, April 11, 1863.

PREFACE.

At the beginning of this war, the only Light Artillery work of any character in circulation was that prepared by a board of United States Artillery officers, and prescribed by the United States government. By the many references to the modifications referring to Horse Artillery (of which there were none at that time in the United States army, and are at this time but three in the Confederate States army—the command of the gallant Pelham), and by the insertion of details respecting it, together with constant references to other movements described in other parts of the book, the explanations of the various manœuvres were found to be complex and confusing. A large quantity of Ordnance matter, useful in its proper place but cumbersome in a book of tactics, was inserted in this work, taken from the United States Ordnance Manual. In the battles before Richmond, where the 1st Maryland Artillery company, under my command, had the high honor, at Mechanicsville, of firing the first gun, the fortune of war threw into my hands a little work on Field Artillery, by Mr. Patten, late officer United States army, published in New York, in November, 1861. This contained every manœuvre of the other, with a clear and simple explanation, complete in itself, without the necessity of reference to other parts of the book, and omitting the details and modifications in reference to Horse Artillery, and met most of the objections to the other work. It possessed over the other a great merit in the engravings, illustrating correctly the several members of the gun detachment, in all the various positions they have respectively to assume while serving and discharging the piece. This was accurately done by means of photography. Valuable as I found this book, it was incomplete—omitting the necessary and essential bugle calls for drill, camp, and field duties. These have been supplied in this work. Since November 1, 1861, the necessities of the service have introduced new guns; the modifications to embrace these have also been supplied, particularly in reference to the light 12-pounder, or Napoleon gun. This gun was introduced by me into the Confederate service—three of them, under an order from Governor Letcher, having been made for me, from drawings furnished by myself, at the Tredegar works, in June and July, 1861, and used at Evansport in the fall and winter of 1861 and 1862. Lately our 6-pounders and 12-pounder howitzers have been or are being recast into Napoleon guns of my pattern—the United States pattern slightly modified.

A few pages referring to the organization, equipment, and management of a mounted battery, and the care and preservation of artillery horses, will, I trust, be useful, though somewhat out of place in a book of tactics. This work agrees in every essential particular with the one prepared by the board of United States officers. It would have been better to have had wood-cut rather than lithographic illustrations, as the cuts would then have been on the same page with the explanations of the various manœuvres The blockade renders this at this time impossible. Whatever of merit there may be in this compilation, the public are for it indebted to the cordial approval of the plan, when suggested by me, by the efficient head of Ordnance Bureau, Colonel JOSIAH GORGAS.

R. SNOWDEN ANDREWS,
Lieutenant-Colonel Commanding Andrews' Battalion Artillery.

Milford, April 1, 1863.

ARTILLERY DRILL.

PART FIRST.

SCHOOL OF THE PIECE.

ARTICLE I.

NOMENCLATURE AND GENERAL PRINCIPLES.

The troops of the Artillery are divided into two kinds, viz: *Foot Artillery*, and *Light* or *Field Artillery*.

To the *Foot Artillery* belong the service of siege, sea-coast, garrison, and mountain artillery, rocket batteries, and the artillery duties of the park.

To the *Field Artillery* belongs the service of *the batteries which manœuvre with the troops on the field of battle.* It is divided into two parts: *Horse Artillery*, which is generally attached to and manœuvres with cavalry, the cannoneers being mounted on horseback, and *Mounted Artillery*, which is generally attached to and manœuvres with infantry, the cannoneers marching at the sides of their pieces, or, when necessary, mounting the ammunition chests. As this last division constitutes the only *Field Artillery* used in the service (except two companies under General J. E. B. Stuart), the instruction in this book will be in reference to *Mounted Artillery* alone.

The Gun.

Figures 1 and 2. The term *Cannon* embraces all kinds of heavy ordnance, GUNS, HOWITZERS, MORTARS; each is mounted on a *carriage,* and each field carriage has a *limber.*

The term PIECE is applied to the *cannon,* and is also used to designate it in union with its carriage, with or without the limber attached.

The *front* of a piece, when *limbered,* or prepared for moving, is the direction in which the pole points; when *unlimbered,* or prepared for action, it is the direction in which the gun points; the *right* and *left* are in each case determined accordingly.

The calibre and description of the pieces now in use in the service of the Confederate States are the 6-pounder and 12-pounder gun; the 12-pounder, 24-pounder, and 32-pounder howitzer; and the 12-pounder *light* gun, or, as it is sometimes called, Napoleon. These are assembled in batteries of six or of eight pieces on the war establishment, of which four or six are guns, and two are howitzers; and of four pieces on the peace establishment, of which *three* are guns and *one* a howitzer. The 12-pounder guns and 24-pounder or 32-pounder howitzers are associated together in the same batteries, which are called 12-*pounder batteries,* and the 6-pounder guns and 12-pounder howitzers are associated together in like manner, and called 6-*pounder batteries.*

Howitzers are cannon formed with chambers for the reception of the cartridge. Figure 2.

The *bore* is the interior hollow cylinder which receives the charge. It includes all the part bored out, viz: the *cylinder,* the *chamber,* if there is one, and the curved surface connecting them. The *bottom of the bore* is a plane surface perpendicular to the *axis*. Its diameter is somewhat less than that of the bore, and is united with the sides by a curved surface. The *muzzle* is the entrance of the bore.

The *breech* is the mass of solid metal between the bottom of the bore and the cascabel. The *seat* for the hausse is behind the *base* of the breech.

The *cascabel* is the projecting part which terminates the piece. It consists of the *knob*, the *neck*, and the *fillet*.

The *reinforce* is the thickest part of the body of the gun.

The *chase* is the conical part of the gun in front of the reinforce.

The *neck* is the smallest part of the piece in front of the *astragal*, or mouldings, at the termination of the chase.

The *swell of the muzzle* is the large part of the gun in front of the neck; it gives strength to the gun at its termination, and facilitates the pointings; the *muzzle sight* is screwed into it. In *field howitzers* a *muzzle band* takes the place of the swell of the muzzle.

The *face* is the front plane terminating the piece.

The *trunnions* are the projecting cylinders at the sides of the gun which support it on its carriage. Their axes are in one line, which is perpendicular to the axis of the bore and in the same plane with it.

The *rimbases* are the short cylinders uniting the trunnions with the body of the gun. Their *ends*, or the *shoulders of the trunnions*, are in planes perpendicular to the axis of the trunnions.

The *vent* is a cylindrical hole, terminating near the bottom of the bore, through which fire is communicated to the charge. It is bored through a *vent piece* of wrought copper, which is screwed into the gun.

The *handles* in heavy field guns are used in the mechanical manœuvres. They are placed, with their centres, over the centre of gravity of the piece.

The Carriage.

Figure 3. The *cheeks* are two pieces of wood between which the gun rests.

The *stock* is of squared wood, in two pieces, joined to the cheeks, and serving to connect the two parts of the carriage together. It is used in directing the piece, etc.

The *trail* is the curved part of the stock, which rests on the ground when the piece is in battery.

The *trunnion plates* are fastened on the cheeks to receive the trunnions.

The *cap squares* are pieces of iron placed over the trunnions to keep them in their plates. They are fastened by chains, pins, and keys.

The *elevating screw* serves to raise or lower the breech. It has a handle with four prongs.

The *lock chain* is placed on the side of the carriage. It serves to keep the wheel from turning.

The *trail handles* are placed on each side of the stock, and serve to raise it.

The *trail plate* is a piece of iron fastened at the trail, having a very stout ring, called the *trail lunette*, which receives the *pintle hook*.

The *pointing rings* (large or small) are on the trail; the large one turns. They receive the handspike.

The *prolonge hooks* are placed on the upper part of the stock. They serve to secure the prolonge when coiled.

The Limber.

The limber is the forward part of the carriage, and runs upon the two fore wheels.

The *axle body* is the wooden part in which the iron *axle-tree* is placed.

The *hounds* are pieces of wood connecting the body of the axle to the *splinter bar,* and upon which the ammunition chest rests.

The *fork* is a piece of wood between the hounds, and forms an opening in which the pole is placed.

The *splinter bar* serves for hitching the wheel-horses, and has for this purpose four *trace hooks.* It is fastened on the hounds and fork.

The *pole straps* guide the pole. They are attached to the harness of the wheel-horses, passing through sliding loops on the breast straps.

The *branches of the pole yoke* are attached by means of sliding rings to the collars of the wheel-horses, and support the pole.

The *pintle hook,* on the hind part of the limber axle-tree, serves to unite the limber to the carriage, and has a key.

The *ammunition chest* serves to transport ammunition, and is placed on the limber.

The Caisson.

It consists of a frame, mounted on wheels, for the transportation of two ammunition chests, a spare wheel, and other spare parts, tools, etc. Its limber is similar to that of the piece. In case of necessity, cannoneers may be transported on the chests.

The *stock* has an iron lunette on the front end; at the rear end it is let in *four* inches for its whole width into the front of the axle body.

The *axle body* is notched to receive the middle rail, and has tenons to fit into notches in the side rails.

The *middle* and two *side rails*, and one *cross bar* complete the wooden parts of the frame.

The *middle assembling bar* (iron) has two *ears* in the middle, to serve as stay plates for the ammunition chests, and a *slat* for the axe-blade on the right of the middle rail.

The *rear assembling bar* supports the spare wheel axle. It has a *slat* on the left of the middle rail for carrying a pickaxe.

The *spare wheel axle* consists of a *body* and *two ribs;* it has a *chain* and *toggle* to secure the wheel. There are *two stays* for the axle; the bolt hole in the head of one of them is square, in the other round.

The *carriage hook* is intended to take a carriage which may have lost its limber.

The *bolster* for the front foot-board is fastened on the middle of the cross bar. The *front foot-board* is fastened to the rails and cross bar; the *rear foot-board* to the rails only.

The *key plate for spare pole* is fastened on the under side of the lunette. The *key* is attached to the left side of the stock by a chain and eye pin, screwed into the left side of the stock. The *spare pole ring* is held by the axle strap.

The *spare handspike ring, key plate,* and *key* are on the right side of the middle rail.

One *key plate* and *key,* for the shovel handle, are fastened on the inside of the right side rail.

The *lock chain bridle* is fastened under the front end of the left side rail; it holds the large ring of the lock chain.

Besides these carriages, a *travelling forge,* with

smiths' and armorers' tools and stores, for shoeing and ordinary repairs, and a *battery wagon* for stores, material, and the tools of the carriage-maker, wheelwright, saddler, and harness-maker, form parts of the battery.

The *battery of manœuvre* consists of the pieces belonging to the field battery, with an equal number of caissons, all properly equipped, horsed, and manned. Each caisson is permanently attached to a piece, and manœuvres with it.

On the war establishment, or when ordered to march, each carriage of the 6-pounder and light 12-pounder batteries is drawn by six horses. On the peace establishment, in garrison, four horses only are required. When 12-pounder batteries are in the field or on the road, each piece and caisson of the battery of manœuvre requires eight horses, the other carriages six horses each.

The Gun Detachment.

The cannoneers of a piece when united for the service of the gun, or for the preliminary instruction, constitute a *detachment*, which is composed ordinarily of eight men, commanded by the gunner.

A *rank* is composed of men abreast; a *file* of men placed one behind the other.

The cannoneers fall in in two ranks, *eighteen* inches between the ranks; elbows slightly touching; and in such manner that they may be told off to the duties at the piece for which they are best fitted. This of course does not apply to recruits, each of whom must be taught the duties of every number under all circumstances.

The gunner tells the detachment off from the right,

No. 1 being on the right of the rear rank, No. 2 on the right of the front rank, No. 3 on the left of No. 1, No. 4 on the left of No. 2, and so on—the even numbers being in the front and the odd numbers in the rear rank. He then takes post on the right of the front rank. The chief of caisson, who, as well as the gunner, should be a corporal, is told off as No. 8 of the gun detachment. When the detachment is composed of more or less than eight men, he should be the highest even number.

When the chief of the piece is present, and not the instructor, he performs the duties and takes the position of the gunner, who then takes post *one* yard in rear of the right file and acts as file-closer, except when the chief of piece is out of ranks, when the gunner resumes his post.

Article II.

METHOD OF INSTRUCTION.

The object of this school is the regular and progressive instruction of the artilleryman in his duties at and connected with the piece, from the period of his joining as a recruit.

This instruction is given by the non-commissioned officers, under the supervision of the chiefs of sections.

The instructor should never require a movement to be performed until it is exactly explained and executed by himself. It should be left to the recruit to take the positions and execute the movements directed, and he should be touched only to rectify mistakes arising from want of intelligence.

Each movement should be perfectly understood

before passing to another. After they have been properly executed in the order laid down, the instructor no longer confines himself to that order.

The instructor allows the men to rest at intervals during drill, and for this purpose he commands *Rest*. At this command the recruit is no longer required to preserve immobility. At the command *Attention*, the man takes his position, and remains motionless.

Great patience and the utmost precision are necessary on the part of the instructor. He should especially endeavor to excite a spirited and active deportment at every military exercise; and, above all, not to disgust the men by too long an application to any one point in the drill.

Article III.

PRELIMINARY INSTRUCTION.

The preliminary instruction to be given to *artillery recruits* is the same as that given to the *infantry soldier*, previous to his instruction in the manual of arms, embracing *the position of the soldier, the facings, and marching*—all of which being fully described in the first part of instruction in infantry tactics need not be repeated here, as reference may be made to that book. Besides this, *artillery recruits* are early instructed in the *sabre exercise*, the details of which are fully explained and illustrated in the compiler's *cavalry drill*, to which work the learner is referred.

In addition to the foregoing, the light artillery soldier should be taught how to mount a horse, and practised at riding, in order that he may be fitted for duties of driver, and any other position requiring a knowledge of horsemanship. He should, moreover, be instructed in the care of horses, and in the manner of harnessing and hitching them.

All of these acquirements are indispensable to the thorough instruction of the artilleryman, though instruction in the schools of the piece and battery need not be delayed to accomplish them.

Article IV.

MANUAL OF THE PIECE.

For the purpose of instruction, each detachment is to be formed in front of the piece, unlimbered, and the different numbers are to be called upon, successively, to perform their respective duties *in detail*, while the rest of the detachment look on and observe their motions. When it is found difficult to make the recruit sensible of the defect in his position, the instructor will place himself or another recruit in the correct position.

Nine men, including the gunner, are necessary for the service of a field piece. When from necessity the detachment consists of less than nine, the higher numbers are struck out and additional duties are imposed upon those remaining.

POSTS OF THE CANNONEERS. PIECE UNLIMBERED.

FIGURE 4. The gunner is at the end of the trail handspike; Nos. 1 and 2 are about *two* feet outside the wheels, No. 1 on the right, and No. 2 on the left; with howitzers, rather in rear of the muzzle; with guns, in line with the front part of the wheels; Nos.

3 and 4 are in line with the knob of the cascabel, covering Nos. 1 and 2; No. 5 is *five* yards in rear of the left wheel; No. 6 in rear of the limber, and No. 7 on his left, covering No. 5; No. 8, the chief of the caisson, is *four* yards in rear of the limber, and on its left; all face to the front.

The chief of the piece is opposite the middle of the trail handspike, outside and near the left cannoneers. In actual firing he takes his place on the right or left, where he can best observe the effect of the shot.

Loading and Firing.

The piece is taken to the drill ground, unlimbered, and prepared for action; the limber in position behind the piece, and facing toward it; the end of the pole *six* yards from the end of the trail handspike.

For the instruction of recruits united for the service of the gun, the exercise is conducted by detail, the instructor giving all the commands. His commands are, *Load by detail*—LOAD; *two, three, four;* SPONGE; *two, three, four;* RAM; *two, three;* READY; FIRE; CEASE FIRING.

When the men are sufficiently instructed to go through the manual without detail, the commands of the instructor for that purpose are, *Load; Commence firing; Cease firing;* or simply, *Commence firing;* and *Cease firing.* After the command *Commence firing* the action is continued as laid down for loading without detail, until the command *Cease firing* is given, which is repeated by the chief of the piece and the gunner.

Duties of the Gunner.

The gunner gives all executive commands in action. He is answerable that all the numbers perform their duties correctly. He communicates the orders which he receives for the kind of ammunition to be fired; sending to No. 6 the time or distance for each round, when firing shells or spherical case shot. He should, when the firing is slow, see that each fuse is properly prepared, and make such corrections as are necessary; for this purpose he, as well as No. 6, should be provided with a fuse gouge.

On receiving the command or signal to commence firing, he gives the command LOAD; takes hold of the handspike at the end with his right hand, and at the centre with his left; places his knee against the left hand, bending over it, the right knee being slightly bent; looks over the top of the piece, and gives the direction. He then steps to the breech to give the elevation, which he does by placing the hausse on its seat, taking hold of a handle of the elevating screw, drawing back his right foot, bending over his left knee, and sighting through the slit in the hausse. (This position is shown in figure 5.)

When the piece is loaded and pointed, he removes the hausse, gives the command READY, and, stepping clear of the wheel to that side where he can best observe the effect of his shot, gives the command FIRE. As soon as the piece has been fired, he causes it to be run up to its former place, if necessary.

When the instructor, instead of giving the command COMMENCE FIRING, gives that of LOAD, the gunner repeats it, and performs the same duties as before, except that he does not command FIRE until the firing is ordered to commence. After the command COMMENCE FIRING is given, the action is continued by the gunner, without further commands from the instructor, until the firing is ordered to cease. When the commands are all given by the instructor, as in *loading by detail*, the gunner performs the same duties, but without repeating the commands.

Duties of No. 1.

Figure 4. Until the command Load, No. 1 stands square to the front, in line with the front part of the wheels, holding the sponge about the middle of the staff in his right hand, and trailing it at an angle of 45°, sponge head up. The instructor commands:

By detail—Load.

Three times and four motions.

Figure 6. At this command No. 1 faces to the left, steps obliquely to the right with his right foot, without moving his left, and at the same time brings the sponge smartly to a perpendicular position by drawing his right hand up in line with the elbow. The sponge is grasped firmly in the hand, and the rammer head kept just over the right toe, the elbow close to the side.

Two.

Figure 7. He steps obliquely to the left with his left foot, planting it about half-way between the piece and the wheel, and opposite the muzzle; bringing the sponge at the same time across his body to the left, so that his right hand may be opposite the middle of the body, the sponge staff being inclined at an angle of 45° across the front of it.

Three.

Figure 8. He takes a side step to the right of *thirty* inches, and, bending his knee, brings the sponge to a horizontal position, extending the hands to the ends of the staff, the sponge head to the left, the back of his right hand up, and that of his left down, the sponge head against the face of the piece.

Four.

FIGURE 9. He inserts the sponge head, drops his left hand behind his thigh, shoulders square, feet equally turned out, straightens the right knee, and, bending over the left, forces the sponge home.

Sponge.

Three times and four motions.

FIGURE 5. At this command No. 1 fixes his eye on the vent to see that it is closed, gives two turns to the sponge, taking great care to press it at the same time against the bottom of the bore.

Two.

FIGURE 10. He draws out the sponge, at the same time straightening his left knee, and bending his right; seizes the staff near the sponge head with his left hand, back of the hand down, and places the sponge against the face of the piece.

Three.

FIGURE 11. He turns the sponge by bringing his hands together in the middle of the staff, giving it a cant with each hand, throwing the sponge head over, at the same time turning his wrist, which brings the staff horizontal, and extending his hands to the ends of the staff, back of the left up, that of the other down.

Four.

Figure 12. He introduces the rammer head into the muzzle as soon as No. 2 has inserted the charge, and joins his left hand to his right, casting his eye to the front.

During the whole time of sponging No. 1 keeps his eye on the vent. If at any time it is not closed, he will discontinue the manœuvre, and command STOP VENT..

Ram.

Two times and three motions.

Figure 13. At this command No. 1 rams home, throwing the weight of his body with the rammer; bending over his left knee, and passing his left arm, with the elbow slightly bent, and back of the hand up, in a horizontal position over the piece, until it points in the direction of the left trunnion; the right shoulder back, and the eyes cast toward the front until the cartridge is home.

Two.

Figure 14. He jerks the sponge out with his right hand, allowing it to slide through the hand as far as the middle of the staff, when he grasps it firmly, and seizing it close to the rammer head with the left hand, back of the hand up, places the rammer head against the face of the piece; both knees straight; eyes to his own front.

Three.

Figure 15. He then draws the sponge close to his body, and immediately steps back outside the wheel, first with the right, then with the left foot, so that when the right foot is brought to it the right hip may be on a line with the front of the wheel. In drawing the right foot to the left he gives the sponge a cant with his left hand, at the same time quitting it, and brings the sponge to a perpendicular position in the right hand, the rammer head resting on the right toe.

READY.

FIGURE 16. At this command, which is given as soon as the piece is loaded, or the firing is about to commence, No. 1 breaks well off to his left with his left foot, bending the left knee and straightening the right leg, drops the end of the sponge staff into the left hand, back of the left down, and fixes his eyes on the muzzle.

The heels should be parallel to the wheels, the body erect on the haunches, and the sponge and hammer held in both hands in a horizontal position, sponge head to the left.

The piece having been fired, No 1 rises on his right knee, and returns to his position, as in the third motion of RAM.

At the command LOAD, he steps in and performs his duties in the same manner as before.

When the loading is not *by detail*, No. 1 goes through all his duties at the command LOAD, returns to his position outside the wheel, as given in the third motion of RAM; breaks off at the command READY, and at the flash of the gun rises, steps in, and performs his duties in the same manner as before. This he continues until the command CEASE FIRING is given, at which command he resumes the position: *To your posts.* If the sponging has been commenced when the command CEASE FIRING is given, it is completed before No. 1 resumes his post.

In sponging and ramming, if the length of the piece requires it, the sponge and rammer are to be pressed home in two motions. No. 1 extending his right hand to the end of the staff as soon as it reaches the muzzle.

In sponging *howitzers*, No. 1 presses the sponge to the bottom of the chamber, which should be well sponged out. He wipes the bore by rubbing its whole surface, without allowing the sponge to turn in his hands.

In the foregoing motions the position of the left foot will not be considered as absolute; it is given as the usual one, and may be modified according to the calibre of the piece and height of the man. The same remarks will apply to the distance between the feet. They will be placed in such position and at such distance from each other as will enable the man to perform his duties with the most ease and steadiness, and at the same time exert his full strength, which will always be required after firing a few rounds, especially when a new sponge is used.

One object of joining the left hand to the right and casting the eyes to the front while ramming, is to refuse the right shoulder; and to secure this object, the left hand, when it passes over the piece, is not carried further back than the direction indicated. This will keep the shoulders in a line parallel with their position at the commencement of the movement until the cartridge is set home, and thus guard against fatal results in case of a premature discharge.

Duties of No. 2.

Until the command LOAD is given, No. 2 remains in his position, shown in figure 4.

On this command being given, he faces to his right, and by two oblique steps, corresponding to those of No. 1, the first with the left, the second at the command Two, with the right foot, he places himself near the muzzle of the piece. At the command THREE, he brings up his left foot to the side of the right, and faces to his right, bringing up his hands together to receive the ammunition from No. 5—the cartridge in the right, the shot in the left hand. Figure 17.

As soon as the sponge is withdrawn he faces to his left, and puts the ammunition into the muzzle, taking care that the seam of the cartridge does not come under the vent, and then steps back, commencing with his left foot, to his position outside the wheel, in the same manner as No. 1 does.

At the command READY, he breaks well off to his right with his right foot, bending the right knee and straightening the left leg; the body erect on the haunches, and fixes his eyes on the muzzle.

The piece having been fired, No. 2 rises on his left leg, remains facing the piece until he hears the command LOAD, or observes the flash of the gun, then steps in, and performs his duty as before. At the command CEASE FIRING, he then takes his position outside the wheel, and faces to the front.

DUTIES OF No. 3.

No. 3 stands in line with the knob of the cascabel, covering No. 1, the priming-wire in his right hand, thumb through the ring, the thumbstall on the left thumb, the tube-pouch fastened to the waist. Fig. 4.

At the command LOAD, he steps to his left, wipes the vent-field with the thumbstall, which he then holds pressed upon the vent, keeping his elbow raised;

his fingers on the left side of the piece, so as to allow the gunner to point over his thumb; the right hand on the tube-pouch. Figure 5.

When the piece is sponged and the charge inserted by No. 2, he jumps to the end of the trail handspike, and, seizing it with both hands, prepares to move it to the right or left on a signal from the gunner, who taps the right of the trail for a movement to the left, and the left of trail for a movement to the right. As soon as the piece is pointed, the gunner raises both hands as a signal to No. 3, who then resumes the position *To your post.*

At the command READY, he steps to the piece, pricks the cartridge, taking care not to move the charge, and covers the vent with his left hand as soon as the tube is inserted. At the command FIRE, he steps to his right, clear of the wheel, and at the flash of the gun, or at the command LOAD, serves vent as before.

No. 3 should be careful to keep the vent closed from the time the sponge enters the muzzle until the charge is inserted by No. 2.

DUTIES OF No. 4.

The post of No. 4 is on a line with the knob of the cascabel, and covering No. 2.

At the command LOAD, No. 4 inserts the lanyard into the ring of a primer, and stands in his position.

At the command READY, he steps in with his right foot, drops the tube in the vent, takes the lanyard in his right hand, moves to the rear so far as to keep the lanyard slack, but capable of being stretched, without altering his position, which should be clear of the wheel, left foot broken to the left and rear. Fig. 18.

At the command FIRE, as soon as No. 3 is clear of the wheel No. 4 pulls the lanyard briskly and firmly, passing the hand, back up, in a downward direction to the rear, so as to keep the lanyard hook from flying back in the direction of the face. Should the tube fail to explode the charge, the gunner immediately commands, *Don't advance, the primer has failed.* Upon which No. 2 steps inside the wheel, close to the axle-tree, receives from No. 3 over the wheel a priming-wire, and from No. 4 a prepared-primer; pricks, primes, and resumes his post. At the command CEASE FIRING, No. 4 secures his lanyard.

No. 3, as well as No. 4, should be equipped with a tube-pouch, furnished with friction-primers and lanyards. In the absence of No. 4, immediately after pricking the cartridge, he prepares and inserts a tube, steps to his post, faces the vent, breaks to his rear with the left foot, and, at the command FIRE, discharges the piece. He then resumes his post, and tends the vent as before.

DUTIES OF NO. 5.

The position of No. 5 is five yards clear of, and covering the left wheel.

At the command LOAD, No. 5 runs to the ammunition chest, receives from No. 7 or No. 6 a single round, the shot in the right hand, the cartridge in his left; takes it to the piece and delivers it to No. 2 (figure 19), returns immediately for another round, and then halts at his post until the piece is fired. In firing shells or spherical case, he exhibits the fuse to the gunner before delivering the charge to No. 2.

Duties of No. 6.

No. 6 is stationed in the rear of the limber chest, and issues the ammunition. He is provided with a fuse gouge, and prepares the shell and spherical case shot according to the distance or time ordered, before delivering it to No. 5.

Duties of No. 7.

The station of No. 7 is in rear of and near the left limber wheel. It is his duty to assist No. 6 in preparation of ammunition, and serving of it to No. 5. In rapid firing, with round shot and canister, Nos. 5 and 7 may alternate in delivering the charges to No. 2, especially when ammunition is issued direct from the caisson.

When the ammunition pouches are used they are worn by Nos. 5 and 7, hung from the left shoulder to the right side; the round is placed in the pouch by No. 6 or No. 7, so that the cartridge will be to the front. When it is brought up No. 5 holds open the pouch, and No. 2 takes out the round with both hands. At the command CEASE FIRING, No. 5 carries the round back to No. 6.

No. 6 will be careful not to raise the lid unnecessarily. It should be kept closed when possible. In firing shells and spherical case, he prepares each fuse as directed, assisted when necessary by No. 7. He gives No. 5 the *time* or *distance* of the fuse with each round issued, who reports to the gunner before delivering it to No. 2. At the command CEASE FIRING, he carefully replaces the ammunition in the chest and secures the lid.

To Cut the Fuse.

Place the projectile between the knees, fuse uppermost, and support it with the left hand. Holding the fuse gouge in the right hand, place the left corner of its edge close to and on the right of the graduated mark indicating the time desired, and cut away gradually until the composition is exposed for a length about equal to the width of the gouge. Great care must be taken not to expose the composition to the left of the proper graduation mark, and to this end particularly avoid *commencing to cut* too close to the desired mark; for after the composition is once exposed it is very easy to pare away to the left, if the time has not been accurately cut. When time permits, it is well to expose the composition fully, either by cutting the opening larger *toward the right* or (with shells only) by cutting another opening to the right of the first. It is in all cases better to enlarge the first opening, and always by extending it toward the right.

Care must be taken not to cut the fuse more rapidly than the demand for shells and shrapnel shot requires.

Moving the Piece by Hand.   Piece Unlimbered.

To the front. The instructor commands:

1. *By hand to the front.* 2. March. 3. Halt.

At the first command the gunner seizes the end of the handspike, and Nos. 1, 2, 3, and 4 the spokes of the wheels; No. 1 with his left hand, Nos. 2, 3, and 4 with both hands; No. 1 holds the sponge with his right hand, the staff resting on his right shoulder, the head down. Figure 20. At the second command they move the piece forward, the gunner raising the trail until the command HALT is given, when all resume their posts.

BY HAND TO THE REAR.

To the rear. The instructor commands:

1. *By hand to the rear.* 2. MARCH. 3. HALT.

At the first command the gunner, facing to the rear, seizes the handspike with his right hand; Nos. 1, 2, 3, and 4 seize the wheels as before, except that No. 1, holding the sponge in the left hand, uses his right at the wheel. At the command MARCH, they move the piece to the rear, the gunner raising the trail, until the command HALT is given, when all resume their posts.

CHANGING POSTS.

In order to instruct the men in all the duties at the piece, the instructor causes them to change posts. For this purpose he commands:

1. *Change posts.* 2. MARCH.

At the command *Change posts*, the men on the right of the piece face to the rear; those who have equipments lay them down, No. 1 resting the sponge head on the nave of the wheel. At the command MARCH, each man takes the place and equipments of the man in his front.

No. 1 takes the place of No. 3.
No. 3   "   "   No. 8.
No. 8   "   "   No. 6.
No. 6   "   "   No. 7.
No. 7   "   "   No. 5.
No 5   "   "   No. 4.
No. 4   "   "   No. 2.
No. 2   "   "   No. 1.

The gunner changes with one of the numbers by special direction of the instructor. A sufficient number of the most intelligent cannoneers must be kept instructed to serve as gunners.

The gunner, who is responsible for the equipments, either distributes them from the limber-chest, or they may be hung on the neck of the cascabel, and distributed by him to the proper numbers at the command Take equipments from the instructor. He receives them again at the command Replace equipments, making such disposition of them as may be directed.

Limbering.

To the front. The instructor commands:

Limber to the front.

At this command No. 1 steps up between the muzzle and the wheel, by the oblique step indicated for loading, turns the staff, seizing it with the left hand, at the same time shifting his right, the back of the right up, that of the left down, and passes the sponge on its hook, rammer head to the rear, to No. 3, who receives the head, secures it against the stop, and keys it up. The piece is then brought about by the cannoneers, and the limber, inclining to the right, passes to its place in front of it, being drawn, when it is not horsed, by Nos. 6 and 7, who take hold at the end of the pole for the purpose.

To bring the piece about, the gunner and No. 5 pass to the right of the handspike, and, facing toward the left, seize it, the gunner near the end, and No. 5 near the middle, and on his right, raise the trail and carry it round to the left; Nos. 1 and 2 bear down upon the muzzle, and Nos. 3 and 4, each using both hands, bring the wheels round, No. 3 turning the right wheel to the rear, and No. 4 the left wheel to the front. When the piece is brought about the trail is lowered; Nos. 3 and 4 step within the wheels, to avoid the limber; Nos. 1 and 2 remain at the muzzle, and the gunner and No. 5 step between Nos. 3 and 4 and the trail, the gunner first taking out the handspike, and passing it to No. 4, by whom it is put up.

As soon as the limber is in front of the piece the gunner commands: HALT; LIMBER UP; upon which the limber halts, the gunner and No. 5 raise the trail by means of the handles, and, assisted by Nos. 3 and 4 at the wheels, and Nos. 1 and 2 at the head of the carriage, run the piece forward, and place the lunette upon the pintle; the gunner then puts in the key, and all take their posts; when necessary, Nos. 6 and 7 assist at the trail in bringing the piece about, and in limbering up.

To the right (or *left*). The instructor commands:

LIMBER TO THE RIGHT (OR LEFT).

The trail is turned to the right (or left), and the piece limbered up as before, the limber inclining to the right (or left), and taking its place by a right (or left) wheel.

To the rear. The instructor commands:

LIMBER TO THE REAR.

The limber inclines to the right, and takes its place by wheeling about to the left, and the piece is then limbered up as before.

Posts of the Cannoneers.   Piece Limbered.

Nos. 1 and 2 are opposite the muzzle; Nos. 3 and 4 opposite the knob of the cascabel; the gunner and No. 5 opposite the rear, and Nos. 6 and 7 opposite the front parts of the limber wheels; No. 8 is on the left, and opposite the limber chest of the caisson. All face to the front, and cover each other in lines *one yard* from the wheels, the even numbers on the right, the odd numbers on the left. The chief of the piece is on the left, and, if not mounted, opposite the end of the pole; if mounted, he is near the leading driver, and on his left.

To Form the Detachment.

To the front.   The instructor commands:

Detachment—front.

The gunner commands: *Cannoneers, forward,* March; the even numbers move directly to the front; the odd numbers closing on them when clear of the piece. The gunner files them to the left, and fronts the detachment at the proper distance. No. 8 moves directly forward, and takes his place in the detachment.

To the rear.   The instructor commands:

Detachment—rear.

The gunner commands: *Cannoneers, rear* face— March. At the command March, the odd numbers move directly to the rear, the even numbers closing on them, and the detachment is filed to the left, halted at a proper distance by the gunner, and faced to the front; No. 8 taking his proper place in the detachment.

In forming detachments in line, they are always, after halting, dressed to the right by the gunner.

Posts of the Detachments at their Pieces.

In front. The detachment is in line facing to the front, *two* yards from the end of the pole or the lead horses.

In rear. The centre of the detachment is *two* yards behind the muzzle, and facing to it.

On the right or left. The detachment is in line opposite the limber axle-tree, and *three* yards from it. In all it faces to the front.

Change of Posts of Detachments at their Pieces.

From front to rear. The detachments being in line, in front of their pieces, to post them in rear, the instructor commands:

Detachments—Rear.

The gunner commands: *Cannoneers, rear* FACE — MARCH. At the command MARCH, Nos. 1, 2, 3, and 4 oblique sufficiently to the left, and Nos. 5, 6, 7, and 8 to the right, move along the sides of their piece, reunite as soon as they have passed it, and are halted at the proper distance, faced to the front, and aligned to the right by the gunner.

From rear to front. The instructor commands:

Detachments—Front.

The gunner repeats the command, and adds — MARCH. At this command the cannoneers oblique: Nos. 1, 2, 3, and 4 to the right; Nos. 5, 6, 7, and 8 to the left; pass their piece, reunite in front, and are halted and aligned to the right by the gunner.

From rear to right (or *left*)   The instructor commands:

DETACHMENTS—RIGHT (OR LEFT).

The gunner commands *right* (or *left*) *oblique*. MARCH, and afterward FORWARD, and HALT, in time to bring the detachment to its post on the right or left. He then aligns it to the right.

TO POST THE CANNONEERS AT THE PIECES LIMBERED.

The detachment being formed in line in front or rear, on the right or left, the instructor commands:

CANNONEERS, TO YOUR POSTS.

From the front. The gunner faces the detachment to the right, and commands: *To your posts*, MARCH. At this command the cannoneers Nos. 1 and 2, turning to the right, and opening out, file to their posts; halt at their proper places, and face to the front.

From the rear, right, or left. At the command CANNONEERS, TO YOUR POSTS, the gunner, in each case, faces the detachment to the left, and marches the cannoneers by that flank to their posts.

POSTS OF THE CANNONEERS ON THE CHESTS.

During the manœuvres the cannoneers are either at their posts or they are seated on the ammunition chests as follows: the gunner and Nos. 5 and 6 on the limber chest of the piece, the gunner on the right and No. 5 on the left; Nos. 1, 2, and 7 on the limber chest of the caisson, No. 2 on the right and No. 1 on the left; Nos. 3, 4, and 8 on the middle chest of the caisson, No. 4 on the right, and No. 3 on the left.

When circumstances require it, Nos. 6 and 7 may

be directed to mount the rear chest of the caisson. They sit with their backs to the front, No. 6 on the right.

To Mount and Dismount the Cannoneers.

To mount. The instructor halts the carriages, if not already at a halt, and commands:

1. *Cannoneers, prepare to mount.* 2. Mount.

At the first command the cannoneers run to their respective places, and stand facing the chests which they are to mount, the gunner and No. 5 in rear of the gun limber, No. 6 on the right of the gunner, Nos. 1 and 2 in rear of the caisson limber, No. 7 on the left of No. 1, Nos. 3 and 4 in front of the middle chest of the caisson, No 8 on the right of No. 3. The gunner and Nos. 2 and 3 seize the handles with the right hand, and step upon the stocks with the left foot, and Nos. 5, 1, and 4 seize the handles with the left hand, and step upon the stocks with the right foot.

At the command Mount, the gunner, and Nos. 1, 2, 3, 4, and 5 spring into their seats. The gunner, and Nos. 5, 1, and 2 seat themselves in their places, with their backs to the front, and immediately face about by throwing their legs outward over the handles.

No. 8 then springs into his seat in the same manner as No. 3; Nos. 6 and 7 step in rear of their chests, place their hands upon them, step upon the stocks with their nearest feet, spring up, step over the boxes, and take their seats, placing their hands on the shoulders of the men already seated in order to steady themselves.

When the command *Cannoneers*, MOUNT is given by itself, the men run to their places and spring into their seats at once, No. 8 taking his seat before No. 3.

To dismount. The instructor halts the carriages as before, and commands:

1. *Cannoneers, prepare to dismount.* 2. DISMOUNT.

At the first command the cannoneers stand up in their places, except the gunner and No. 5, who face about. At the second command the whole jump off and run to their posts.

When the command *Cannoneers*, DISMOUNT is given by itself, the men jump from their chests in the same manner.

The cannoneers always dismount at the command ACTION FRONT, RIGHT, or LEFT. They also dismount at the command IN BATTERY, as soon as the carriage on which they are mounted halts.

The object of mounting the cannoneers on the ammunition chests is generally to enable the battery to make quick movements. Care should be taken when the ground is unfavorable, or the movements are likely to be prolonged, not to mount them so often as to be injurious to the horses. After they are well instructed in mounting and dismounting at a halt, the cannoneers may be ordered to mount and dismount while the carriages are in march at a walk.

When a caisson is absent, or temporarily disabled, and a quick movement is necessary, Nos. 1, 2, and 3 will mount the off-horses of the piece, No. 2 the lead, No. 1 the middle, and No. 3 the wheel-horse, Nos. 1 and 3 passing by the rear of the gun. This arrangement may also be resorted to in case of a sudden alarm, the drivers of the caissons assisting the drivers of the pieces by harnessing their off-horses and hitching them in. The cannoneers then mount as directed, and the pieces move off. The remaining cannoneers assist the drivers of the caissons to harness and hitch in their horses, and then mount the chests of the caissons, which proceed at once to join their pieces.

MOVING THE PIECE BY HAND. PIECE LIMBERED.

To the front. The instructor commands:

    1. FORWARD. 2. MARCH. 3. HALT.

At the first command Nos. 6 and 7 seize the end of the pole with both hands, the gunner and No. 5 facing toward the pole, seize the splinter bar with one hand and the pole with the other; Nos. 3 and 4 seize the spokes of the hind wheels with both hands, and Nos. 1 and 2 apply both hands at the head of the carriage. At the second command all, acting together, urge the piece forward until the command HALT is given, when all resume their posts. Figure 21.

Moving the Piece by Hand.

To the rear. The instructor commands:

    1. BACKWARD. 2. MARCH. 3. HALT.

At the first command all face to the rear; Nos. 6 and 7 seize the end of the pole with both hands; No. 5 and the gunner seize the spokes of the limber, and Nos. 1, 2, 3, and 4 those of the hind wheels. At the command MARCH, all, moving together, move the piece to the rear, Nos. 6 and 7 keeping it straight by the use of the pole. At the command HALT, all resume their posts.

Unlimbering and Coming into Action.

To the front. The instructor commands:

Action front.

At this command the gunner takes out the key, and, assisted by No. 5, raises the trail from the pintle, and then commands Drive on, upon which Nos. 6 and 7 reverse the limber to the left, and proceed with it to the rear; again reverse to the left, and halt so that the limber shall cover the piece, with the end of the pole *six* yards from the end of the trail handspike. At the same time that the limber moves off the piece is brought about in all respects as in limbering to the front, except that the gunner and No. 5, without lowering the trail, carry it about, each by means of the handle on his own side. Nos. 6 and 7, when necessary, assist at the trail, after placing the limber in position.

As soon as the piece is brought about, and the trail lowered, No. 4 takes out the handspike and passes it to the gunner, who fixes it in the trail. No. 1 takes out the sponge, No. 3 unkeying it, and No. 4 prepares his lanyard. All then resume their posts.

To the right (or *left*). The instructor commands:

Action right (or left).

The piece is unlimbered and placed in the required direction, and the limber wheels to the left (or right), and takes its place in rear, by reversing to the left (or right).

To the rear. The instructor commands:

1. *Fire to the rear.* 2. In battery.

At the command In battery, the piece is unlimbered as before, the trail immediately lowered, and the gun prepared for action. The limber moves directly forward at the command DRIVE ON from the gunner, and takes its place by coming to the left about.

SERVICE OF THE GUN WITH DIMINISHED NUMBERS.

The men should be frequently exercised in serving pieces with diminished numbers, that each may know the duties he has to perform in such cases.

Disabled men are replaced as soon as possible by the highest numbers, or, if men are selected to replace them, the highest numbers will be reduced to fill the vacancies thus created. During action, Nos. 1 and 2 may occasionally change places and numbers, as the duties of No. 1 are very severe.

Service of the gun by two men. The gunner commands, points, serves the vent, and fires; No. 1 sponges, loads, and serves ammunition.

Three men. The gunner commands, points, serves the vent, and fires; No. 1 sponges; No. 2 loads, and serves ammunition.

Four men. The gunner commands and points; No. 1 sponges; No. 2 loads, and serves ammunition; No. 3 serves the vent, and fires.

Five men. The gunner commands and points; No. 1 sponges; No. 2 loads; No. 3 serves the vent, and fires; No. 4 serves ammunition.

Six men. The gunner commands and points; No. 1 sponges; No. 2 loads; No. 3 serves the vent, and fires; Nos. 4 and 5 serve ammunition.

Seven men. The gunner commands and points; No. 1 sponges; No. 2 loads; No. 3 serves the vent, and attends to the trail; No. 4 fires; No. 6 is at the limber, serves ammunition to No. 5, and occasionally changes with him.

Eight men. No. 7 assists No. 6; the other numbers as before.

TABLE FOR THE EXERCISE WITH DIMINISHED NUMBERS.

Nos. Retained.	Distribution of Duties.							
	Gunner.	1	2	3	4	5	6	7
G. 1	G. 3, 4	1,2,5	....	....	....	....	....	....
G. 1, 2	G. 3, 4	1	2, 5	....	....	....	....	....
G. 1, 2, 3	G.	1	2, 5	3, 4	....	....	....	....
G. 1, 2, 3, 4	G.	1	2	3, 4	5	....	....	....
G. 1, 2, 3, 4, 5	G.	1	2	3, 4	6	5	....	....
G. 1, 2, 3, 4, 5, 6	G.	1	2	3	4	5	6	....
G. 1, 2, 3, 4, 5, 6, 7 ..	G.	1	2	3	4	5	6	7

SUPPLY OF AMMUNITION IN ACTION.

When it is likely that movements must take place on the field, or the firing is slow, and it can be done without inconvenience, ammunition will be served direct from the rear chest of the caisson, No. 8 performing the duties prescribed for No. 6 at the limber chest. At convenient moments the ammunition served out by No. 6 will be replaced from the rear caisson chest.

ARTICLE IV.

MECHANICAL MANŒUVRES.

CHANGING WHEELS.

Napoleon, 6-pounder gun, and 12-pounder howitzer. The piece being unlimbered, to change the right wheel, the instructor commands:

1. *Prepare to change the right wheel.* 2. CHANGE THE WHEEL.

At the first command Nos. 5, 6, and 7 dismount the spare wheel; No. 5 brings it near, and parallel to the disabled one, leaving room for the latter to be taken off. The gunner passes one end of his handspike to No. 1, placing it under the axle-tree close to the shoulder. The gunner and No. 1, placing themselves between the handspike and piece, and facing the wheel, take hold of the handspike near the axle; Nos. 4 and 6 take hold of the ends of the handspike, No. 6 assisting the gunner.

At the command CHANGE THE WHEEL, the carriage is raised; Nos. 2 and 3 take off the disabled wheel; No. 2 runs it to the rear, and Nos. 3 and 5 put on the spare wheel, No. 3 taking hold of it in the rear. Nos. 3 and 4 attend to the linchpins and washers on their respective sides.

To change the left wheel, the gunner and No. 2, assisted by Nos. 6 and No. 3 respectively, man the handspike; Nos. 1 and 4 take off the wheel; Nos 5, 6, and 7 dismount the spare wheel; No. 5 brings it up, and Nos. 4 and 5 put it on; No. 1 runs the disabled wheel to the rear.

The men at the handspike must raise the end of the axle-tree sufficiently high to throw the weight on the other wheel, and those who take off the wheel must also lift it, and not increase the weight by allowing it to slide along the axle-tree.

12-pdr. gun and 24-pdr. howitzer. One end of a prolonge is fastened to the axle-tree near the disabled wheel, the other end being passed over the opposite wheel, and manned by four men from another piece. A spare pole, manned by Nos. 1, 2, 3, 4, 5, and 6, must be substituted for the handspike under the axle-tree. The gunner and No. 7 take off and put on the wheels. When a spare pole can not be obtained, the carriage may be raised by means of the handspikes; No. 2 places one in the muzzle, and No. 1 crosses the other under it; No. 3 assists at the handspike in the muzzle, and Nos. 4, 5, and 6 at the other, No. 4 on the outside. The four men from the other piece take hold of the cheeks on the side to be raised. All, acting together, raise the carriage at the command CHANGE THE WHEEL. The prolonge is not required. The manœuvre would be made easier by digging a trench five or six inches deep for the other wheel.

When a wheel at the piece is disabled in action, it may be replaced by one from its limber. The disabled wheel, if not quite unserviceable, may be used at the limber until it can be conveniently changed; but, if entirely unserviceable, one must be obtained from the caisson as soon as it is possible to bring it up.

In taking off a limber wheel the horses are taken out; No. 6 removes the linchpin and washer; Nos. 3 and 4, assisted by Nos. 7 and 8, raise the limber, No. 3 in front and No. 4 in rear of the axle-tree; Nos. 5 and 6 take off the wheel, and No. 5 runs it forward. The axle-tree is lowered gently to the ground.

The wheel of the limber is replaced by Nos. 1, 2, 5, and 6 after the wheel of the piece is on, Nos. 1 and 2 raising the limber, assisted by Nos. 7 and 8.

When a wheel has been disabled in the carriage of either piece or caisson, and can not be replaced by another, a spar ten or twelve feet long may be placed under the axle-tree, with one end resting on the ground and the other secured to the carriage by lashing, so that the axle-tree may be supported in its proper position without the wheel. The part of the carriage thus supported should be relieved of as much weight as possible.

When a wheel has been so disabled that it can not turn, a shoe of wood may be made and placed under it. A piece of spar about three feet long and nine inches in diameter, with a groove in one side to receive the felloe, will answer for this purpose. The end in front is given the proper form, and the lock chain fastened to it. In this case, also, the carriage should be relieved from as much weight as possible.

Dismounting Pieces.

Napoleon, 6-pdr. gun and 12-pdr. howitzer. The piece being unlimbered, the instructor commands:

1. *Prepare to dismount the piece.* 2. Dismount the piece.

At the first command Nos. 1, 2, 3, and 4 remove the implements and place them on the ground, outside of their respective wheels, the bucket with a sponge and handspike on the right, and the worm with a sponge and handspike on the left. Nos. 1 and 2 then press upon the muzzle, and Nos. 3 and 4, after removing the cap squares, station themselves at the end of the cheeks, and, with one hand on the wheel and the other on the knob of the cascabel, prepare to raise the breech. The gunner, first taking out the handspike, if in the trail, and passing it to No. 4, raises the elevating-screw to its greatest height, and then seizes the left trail handle; No. 5 seizes the right, and Nos. 6 and 7, after scotching the wheels, go to the trail to assist in raising it.

At the second command Nos. 1 and 2 bear down upon the muzzle, the gunner and Nos. 5, 6, and 7 raise the trail until the muzzle rests upon the ground, No. 5, with the howitzer, holding the lock chain to prevent the chain from falling over to the front. Nos. 3 and 4 push against the cascabel to raise the breech, and, when the piece is vertical, run around to assist Nos. 1 and 2 to keep it in that position. The trail is then lowered, the carriage run back, and the piece placed on the ground, vent upward. The cannoneers then replace the implements, Nos. 3 and 4 securing the cap squares.

12-pdr. gun and 24-pdr. howitzer. These are dismounted in the same manner, except that Nos. 1 and 2 make a hole in the ground under the head of the carriage, one foot deep for the 12-pdr., and eight inches for the howitzer, to receive the muzzle, and they are assisted by two additional men in pressing upon the muzzle and in steadying the piece.

By attaching the middle of a rope with an artificer's knot to the knob of the cascabel, and hauling upon the ends of it, the piece may be more securely steadied. Nos. 3 and 4 attach the rope, pass the ends over to Nos. 1 and 2, and then go around to assist them in hauling. Four additional men from another piece also assist. When the trail is raised so as to let the muzzle touch the bottom of the hole, the men haul upon the rope and disengage the gun, Nos. 1, 2, 3, and 4 coming up hand over hand to steady it.

A rope may also be used in dismounting the 6-pdr. gun and 12-pdr. howitzer. Nos. 1 and 2 man the rope, and Nos. 3 and 4 steady the wheels. No additional men are required.

Mounting Pieces.

6-pdr. gun and 12-pdr. howitzer. The piece being on the ground, vent upward, the instructor commands:

1. *Prepare to mount the piece.* 2. MOUNT THE PIECE.

At the first command the implements are removed as in dismounting, except that the handspikes, instead of being placed on the ground, are passed by Nos. 3 and 4 respectively to the gunner and No. 2; Nos. 3 and 4 take off the cap squares; No. 2 inserts his handspike in the bore, and, assisted by No. 1, raises the chase, so that the gunner may put his handspike under the piece a little in rear of the trunnions.

This being done, No. 2 withdraws his handspike from the bore, and places it under the knob of the cascabel. Nos. 1, 3, and 4 assist at the handspike of No. 2, and Nos. 5, 6, and 7 at that of the gunner; Nos. 1, 2, 5, and the gunner being at the ends. The gunner then commands HEAVE, upon which the men, acting together, raise the piece upright, and Nos. 1, 2, 3, and 4 steady it in that position. The gunner and No. 5 go to the trail, and, assisted by 6 and 7 at the wheels, run the carriage forward within a foot of the piece. Nos. 6 and 7 scotch the wheels, if necessary, and then go to the trail to assist the gunner and No. 5 in raising it.

At the second command the trail is raised, No. 5, with the howitzer, holding the lock chain to prevent the trail from falling over to the front; Nos. 1 and 2 push gently against the piece, and place the trunnions in their plates. The trail is then lowered carefully to the ground, the wheels unscotched, and the implements replaced, Nos. 3 and 4 securing the cap squares. When necessary, the duties of Nos. 6 and 7 can be performed by Nos. 3 and 4.

The piece may be also easily raised by means of a rope, without the use of handspikes. The gunner fixes the middle of the rope to the knob of the cascabel by an artificer's knot, and Nos. 1, 2, 3, 4, 5, and 6 man the ends, Nos. 1 and 2 being nearest the cascabel. By hauling upon the rope the piece is raised. It is then mounted as before.

12-pdr. gun and 24-pdr. howitzer. These are mounted by means of handspikes in the same manner as the 6-pdr. gun and 12-pdr. howitzer, except that Nos. 1 and 2 make a hole in the ground, one foot deep for the 12-pdr., and eight inches for the howitzer, to receive the muzzle, and two additional men act at the handles.

It will facilitate the raising of the piece, and give greater security, to fasten the handspike to the cascabel by means of a rope, and also to fasten, by an artificer's knot, the middle of a prolonge or picket rope to the cascabel, and man the ends of it by men from another piece. In this case, when the piece is raised as high as the man's hips, the gunner and Nos. 5, 6, and 7 quit the handspike, two at a time, and assist at the prolonge. In placing the piece on the carriage, Nos. 3 and 4 carry the prolonge to the rear, and assist by hauling upon it. When the piece does not fall exactly into the trunnion plates, the prolonge is passed round under the cheeks to secure the breech to the carriage; the tail being then lowered, the trunnions slide into their beds.

CARRYING PIECES.

The piece being on the ground, vent upward, the instructor commands:

1. *Prepare to carry the piece.* 2. FORWARD. 3. MARCH.

At the first command Nos. 6 and 7 back the limber over the breech until the pintle-hook is just above the trunnions; No. 2 inserts a handspike in the bore to raise the piece, and Nos. 1, 3, and 4 stand near to assist him; the gunner, assisted by No. 5, passes the ring of the prolonge through the handles, and, after making a turn with the prolonge round the pintle-hook, passes the ring through the handles again and puts it on the pintle. If there are no handles, the prolonge should be passed round the piece, in front and rear of the trunnions, the piece being raised for that purpose. Nos. 6 and 7 then raise the pole, and Nos. 1, 2, 3, and 4 the piece, if not already raised; the gunner tightens the prolonge, pulling on the free end, which he passes over the pintle-hook and under the limber to No. 5, who receives it at the splinter bar, and makes a turn with it round the fork. The pole is then lowered, and Nos. 1 and 2 press upon the muzzle and raise the breech. The gunner, assisted by No. 5, lashes the knob of the cascabel to the splinter bar, fastening the end of the prolonge by half-hitches. The piece when slung should be horizontal.

At the second command the cannoneers prepare to move the limber forward.

At the command MARCH, they move the limber to the front.

When the horses are hitched in, they should be taken out to enable the men to sling the piece.

A limber, in addition to carrying the piece, may also carry a disabled carriage when it is taken apart and lashed upon it; but, as the weight when so distributed is too great to be carried far, the carriage should be placed upon the caisson as soon as it can be done.

When a limber is disabled, the trail of the carriage or caisson is attached to the rear of another carriage.

DISMOUNTING CARRIAGES.

Carriages of the 6-pdr. gun and 12-pdr. howitzer. The piece being dismounted and implements taken off, as already described, the instructor commands:

1. *Prepare to dismount the carriage.* 2. DISMOUNT THE CARRIAGE.

At the first command Nos. 3 and 4 remove the linchpins and washers, and Nos. 1, 2, 3, and 4 step inside of the wheels and take hold of the carriage.

At the second command Nos. 1, 2, 3, and 4 lift the carriage, Nos. 5 and 7 take off the right wheel, and Nos. 6 and 8 the left; Nos. 5 and 6 taking hold in front, and Nos. 7 and 8 in rear.

If necessary, each wheel may be taken off by one man.

The carriages of the 12-pdr. gun and 24-pdr. howitzer are dismounted in the same manner, with the addition of two or four men to assist in lifting the carriages.

Limbers. The limbers are dismounted in the same manner as the carriages; the different numbers taking hold in the same relative positions, and performing the same duties.

MOUNTING CARRIAGES.

The method of mounting carriages and limbers corresponds to that of dismounting them.

CHANGING AMMUNITION CHESTS.

In service, when the limber-chest of the piece is emptied, the piece and caisson exchange limbers; No. 8, assisted by No. 7, unlimbers and limbers up the caisson, and the middle chest is exchanged with the empty one on the limber as soon as practicable.

To change the ammunition chests, the instructor commands:

1. *Prepare to change the ammunition chest.* 2. CHANGE THE CHEST.

At the first command Nos. 5 and 6 unkey the empty chest, each on his own side, and, taking hold of the handles, place it upon the ground, on the left of the caisson. Nos. 7 and 8 unkey the middle chest at the same time.

At the command CHANGE THE CHEST, Nos. 5, 6, 7, and 8, seizing the middle chest by the handles, lift it on the foot-board, and, turning it end for end there, shift the chest along the stock to the limber, taking great care not to cut the bottom on the nuts, and put it in place; Nos. 5 and 6 resume their posts immediately; Nos. 7 and 8 key the chest, replace the empty chest, key it, and resume their posts.

RIGHTING CARRIAGES THAT HAVE BEEN OVERTURNED.

When a carriage has been overturned, it is better, if time permits, to disengage the piece, right the carriage, and then mount the piece again in the manner already described. The piece may be easily disengaged by allowing the breech to rest upon the ground, or a block of wood, raising the muzzle by means of a handspike, while the cap squares are taken off.

The carriage may be righted, however, without disengaging the piece, by the following modes:

1st. Detach the limber, secure the cap squares, and lash the knob of the cascabel to the stock. Place the middle of a rope over the nave of one wheel, pass the ends of it downward between the lower spokes of that wheel, then under the carriage, through the corresponding spokes of the other wheel, and then upward over the wheel, and across the top of the carriage, to the side where it was first attached. The ends of the rope and the wheel to be raised are then manned, and the carriage drawn over to its upright position. During this operation two men are required to steady the trail.

If necessary, the ends of the rope may be fastened to the limber, and horses used to assist in righting the carriage. Great care must be taken to stop the horses in time, and to prevent them from making any more effort than is absolutely necessary. If the wheel-horses are sufficient the leaders may be unhitched.

2d. Detach the limber, attach two prolonges, or the middle of a picket rope, to the trail, chock the wheels, and dig an oblong hole under the muzzle, about two and a half feet deep. Then pass one of the prolonges, or one end of the picket rope, over the carriage to the front, and, manning both, raise the trail, and pass it over the axle-tree to the ground on the opposite side.

Light carriages may be righted by hand without attaching a rope.

SPIKING AND UNSPIKING CANNON, AND RENDERING THEM UNSERVICEABLE.

To spike a piece, or to render it unserviceable. Drive into the vent a jagged and hardened steel spike with a soft point, or a nail without a head; break it off flush with the outer surface, and clinch the point inside by means of the rammer. Wedge a shot in the bottom of the bore by wrapping it with felt, or by means of iron wedges, using the rammer or a bar of iron to drive them in; a wooden wedge would be easily burnt by means of a charcoal fire lighted with the aid of a bellows. Cause shells to burst in the bore of brass guns, or fire broken shot from them with high charges. Fill a piece with sand over the charge to burst it. Fire a piece against another, muzzle to muzzle, or the muzzle of one to the chase of the other. Light a fire under the chase of a brass gun, and strike on it with a sledge to bend it. Break off the trunnions of iron guns; or burst them by firing them with heavy charges and full of shot at a high elevation.

When guns are to be spiked temporarily, and are likely to be retaken, a *spring spike* is used, having a shoulder to prevent its being too easily extracted.

To unspike a piece. If the spike is not screwed in or clinched, and the bore is not impeded, put in a charge of powder of one-third of the weight of the shot, and ram junk wads over it with a handspike, laying on the bottom of the bore a strip of wood with a groove on the under side, containing a strand of quick match, by which fire is communicated to the charge. In a brass gun, take out some of the metal at the upper orifice of the vent, and pour sulphuric acid into the groove for some hours before firing. If this method, several times repeated, is not successful, unscrew the vent-piece, if it be a brass gun, and, if an iron one, drill out the spike or drill a new vent.

To drive out a shot wedged in the bore. Unscrew the vent-piece, if there be one, and drive in wedges so as to start the shot forward, then ram it back in order to seize the wedge with a hook; or pour in powder and fire it, after replacing the vent-piece. In the last resort, bore a hole in the bottom of the breech, drive out the shot, and stop the hole with a screw.

Article V.

POINTING AND RANGES.

To point a piece is to place it in such a position that the shot may reach the object it is intended to strike. To do this, the axis of the trunnions, being horizontal, the line of metal, called also the natural line of sight, must be so directed as to pass through the object, and then the elevation given to the piece to throw the shot the required distance. The *direction* is given from the trail, and the *elevation* from the breech; the trail being traversed by a handspike, and the breech raised or depressed by an elevating-screw.

The *axis of the piece* coincides with that of the cylinder of the bore.

The *line of sight* in pointing is the line of direction from the eye to the object. It lies in a vertical plane, passing through, or parallel to, the axis of the piece.

The *angle of sight* is the angle which the line of sight makes with the axis of the piece.

The *natural line of sight* is the straight line passing through the highest points of the base ring and the swell of the muzzle, muzzle sight, or muzzle band.

The *natural angle of sight* is the angle which the *natural* line of sight makes with the axis of the piece.

The *dispart of a piece* is half the difference between the diameters of the base ring and swell of the muzzle, or the muzzle band. It is therefore the tangent of the natural angle of sight to a radius equal to the distance from the highest point of the swell of the muzzle or muzzle band to the plane passing through the rear of the base ring.

By *range* is commonly meant the distance between the piece and the object which the ball is intended to strike; or the first graze of the ball upon the horizontal plane on which the carriage stands. *Point-blank range* is the distance between the piece and the point-blank. *Extreme range* is the distance between the piece and the spot where the ball finally rests.

Theory of pointing. The point-blank is the second point of intersection of the trajectory or curve described by the projectile in its flight with the line of sight. As the angle of sight is increased the projectile is thrown farther above the line of sight, and the trajectory and point-blank distance becomes more extended.

The point-blank range increases with the *velocity*, the *diameter*, and the *density* of the ball. It is also affected by the inclination of the line of sight; but with the angles of elevation used in field service this effect is too small to be taken into account.

A piece is said to be aimed *point-blank* when the line of metal, which is the natural line of sight, is directed upon the object. This must be the case when the object is at point-blank distance. When at a greater distance, the pendulum-hausse or the tangent scale is raised upon the breech until the sight is at the height which the degree of elevation for the distance may require. An artificial line of sight and an *artificial* point-blank are thus obtained, and the piece is aimed as before.

The different lines, angles, etc., which an artilleryman has to take into account when pointing, will be best understood by the following figure:

E P c G is the axis of the piece. P g D is the trajectory or curve described by the projectile in its flight. A B c F is the natural line of sight. A c E is the natural angle of sight.

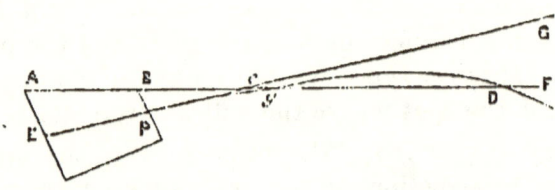

The projectile, thrown in the direction of the axis E P c G, is acted upon by the force of gravity, and begins to fall at once below the line at the rate of $16\frac{1}{2}$ feet for one second, $64\frac{1}{3}$ for two, $144\frac{3}{4}$ for three, and so on in proportion to the time. It cuts the line of sight at G, a short distance from the muzzle of the piece, and, descending, again cuts it at the point D. This second point of intersection is the *point-blank*.

Pendulum-hausse. The instrument at present in most general use in pointing field guns at objects beyond the natural point-blank, is called a *pendulum-hausse*, of which the component parts are denominated the *scale*, the *slider*, and the *seat*. The *scale* is made of sheet brass: at the lower end is a brass bulb filled with lead. The *slider* is of thin brass, and is retained in any desired position on the scale by means of a brass set-screw with a milled head. The scale is passed through a slit in a piece of steel, with which it is connected by a brass screw, forming a pivot on which the scale can vibrate laterally: this slit is made long enough to allow the scale to take a vertical position in any *ordinary* cases of inequality of the ground on which the wheels of the carriage may stand. The ends of this piece of steel form two journals, by means of which the scale is supported on the *seat* attached to the piece, and is at liberty to vibrate in the direction of the axis of the piece. The *seat* is of iron, and is fastened to the base of the breech by three screws, in such manner that the centres of the two journal notches shall be at a distance from the axis equal to the radius of the base ring.

A *muzzle sight* of iron is screwed into the swell of the muzzle of *guns*, or into the middle of the muzzle ring of *howitzers*. The height of this sight is equal to the *dispart* of the piece, so that a line from the *top* of the muzzle sight to the *pivot* of the scale is parallel to the axis of the piece. Consequently, the vertical plane of sight passing through the centre line of the scale and top of the muzzle sight will be also parallel to the axis in any position of the piece: the scale will therefore always indicate correctly the angle which the line of sight makes with the axis. The *seat* for suspending the hausse upon the piece is adapted to each piece according to the varying inclination of the base of the breech to the axis. The *hausse*, the *seat*, and the *muzzle sight*, varying as they do in their construction and arrangement, according to the configuration of the piece upon which they are intended to be used, are marked for the kind of piece to which they belong. The graduations on the scale are the tangents of each quarter of a degree to a radius equal to the distance between the muzzle sight and the centre of the journal-notches, which are, in all cases, one inch in rear of the base ring.

The hausse, when not in use, is carried by the gunner in a leather pouch, suspended from a shoulder-strap.

Part Second.

SCHOOL OF THE BATTERY.

Article I.

GENERAL PRINCIPLES.

The manœuvres of a field battery are intended to furnish the instruction required for conducting its movements and formations in all situations in which it can be employed.

The movements are described for one flank only. They may be executed by the other flank according to the same principles, and by inverse means.

The battery of manœuvre is divided into sections, each being composed of two pieces and two caissons. The column of sections is not only found to be sufficient for the purpose of manœuvre, but much more convenient than the column of pieces or half-batteries. The column of pieces requires too great an extension of the battery, and too much time for its evolutions. In the column of half-batteries one chief of section is deprived of his command; and, when formed at full distance, the depth of the column is essentially the same as that of sections. Moreover, when this column is used for manœuvre, the pieces of the same section can not be kept long together in any part of the battery. These objections to the column of half-batteries do not, however, apply to the eight-gun battery, which can be manœuvred by half-batteries without depriving a chief of section of his command, or separating the pieces of the same section. Habitually, this battery will be manœuvred by sections, but when necessary, or expedient, it may be manœuvred by half-batteries.

Each piece and its caisson are kept in a fixed relation to each other, and may be said to constitute a unit. They are separated only in the formations in battery. This principle simplifies the manœuvres greatly, and renders it generally unnecessary to give separate commands to the caissons.

No notice is taken of inversions in any of the orders, either in column, in line, or in battery. The most simple and rapid formations are always adopted.

The passage of carriages is used as an elementary principle in the manœuvres. In the formations in battery it is indispensable for changing the front of a line; and when executed seasonably, as a preparatory movement, it greatly facilitates all the formations. It may be executed with the same, or an increased gait.

But one wheel is admitted. The pivot carriage preserves its gait, while the others regulate theirs according to their distances from it; the guide being always on the pivot flank.

No general or special guides are used. The chiefs of pieces are the guides of the carriages to which they are attached. And each becomes the guide of the line or column whenever his carriage occupies the position to which the movements are referred.

The cautionary command *Attention* is not embraced among those required for the manœuvres, but may be used at the discretion of the captain. The commands of the chiefs of sections are more numerous, and those of the captain are more frequently repeated, than in other arms of service, on account of the noise of carriages and extent of command.

As a general rule, the cannoneers should mount the ammunition chests only for rapid movements; and when within range of the enemy's guns, they should dismount, unless important considerations require a continuation of the rapid gait. The explosion of a caisson when the cannoneers are mounted might destroy many men.

Two methods have been adopted for the formations in battery to the front: one requiring the pieces to be thrown forward, the other requiring the caissons to be thrown to the rear. The first method is equally adapted to light and heavy batteries. By this method the pieces and caissons are rapidly separated; and the commands may be given while the battery is moving, so as to leave the caissons at their proper distance in rear of the line on which the pieces are to form. The second method is not adapted to heavy batteries, on account of the difficulty of turning the pieces about by hand. But with light pieces it is advantageous when the battery is already formed upon the line of battle, or when the head of the column which is to be formed into battery is very near that line.

Composition of the Battery of Manœuvre.

The *Battery of Manœuvre* is composed of six field pieces and six caissons, properly manned, horsed, and equipped. It is sometimes reduced to four, or increased to eight pieces. The tactics are adapted to either number, but six pieces are supposed.

Each carriage is drawn by four or six horses, and the officers and men are as follows:

One captain, who commands the battery.

Three lieutenants, each commanding a section; the section of the junior lieutenant should be in the centre.

One lieutenant, commanding the line of caissons.

When half-batteries are formed, they are commanded by the two lieutenants highest in rank.

Six mounted sergeants, each charged with guiding and superintending a piece.

Twenty-four or thirty-six drivers, being one to each pair of horses.

Six detachments of cannoneers, each containing nine men. This number includes two corporals, one of whom is chief of the caisson; and the other, the gunner, has charge of the gun and its detachment.

Two trumpeters or buglers.

One guidon.

The battery is divided into three sections, denominated the right, left, and centre sections. Should there be four sections, they are denominated the *right, right-centre, left-centre,* and *left* sections. A section contains two pieces and two caissons, and in each section the pieces are denominated *right piece* and *left piece*.

The battery is also divided into half-batteries, denominated *right half-battery* and *left half-battery*.

The word *piece* applies to the gun or howitzer, either with or without its limber; and sometimes to the piece and caisson together.

The *front of a battery,* in the order in battery, is the front of the line of pieces. In all other formations it is the front of the first line of drivers.

The *right* or *left* of a battery is always that of the actual front, whether the pieces or caissons lead.

The *interval* is a space measured parallel to the front.

The *distance* is a space measured in depth, or perpendicular to the front.

The *measures* of intervals and distances are given in yards, and express the vacant spaces between the component parts of the battery.

FIGURE 22. The object of *a right or left wheel* is to give the carriage a direction perpendicular to the one it had before. In executing it, the leading horse on the pivot flank describes a quadrant (*five* yards) of a circle whose radius is 3.25 yards, and then resumes the direct march. The horse coupled to him increases his gait and conforms to his movement, resuming the direct march at the same time. The centre and wheel horses follow in the tracks of their leaders.

FIGURE 23. The object of *a right or left oblique* is to give the carriage a direction inclined 45° to the right or left of the one it had before. In executing it, the leading horse on the pivot flank describes the eighth of a circle, whose radius is 3.25 yards, and then resumes the direct march. The horse coupled to him increases his gait, conforms to his movement, and resumes the direct march at the same time. The other horses follow in the tracks of their leaders. The oblique of a carriage is in fact one-half of a right or left wheel.

FIGURE 24. The *passage* applies to two carriages in file, and its object is to pass the rear carriage to the front. To execute it, the rear carriage inclines to the right, passes the one in front, and takes its proper distance in front by inclining to the left. The reciprocal gaits of the carriages are regulated by commands.

FIGURE 25. The object of an *about* is to establish the carriage on the same ground, but in the opposite direction, having the heads of the leading horses where the hinder part of the carriage was before. For the easy execution of this movement at all gaits, and with a carriage of four wheels, all the horses incline at once to the right as they advance, and so move, according to their distances from the pole, as not to interfere with the wheel-horses, which really govern the carriage.

FIGURE 26. The *countermarch* applies to two carriages of different kinds in file. Its object is to make them both perform the about, and to establish them on the ground they occupied before, but in the opposite direction and with the same carriage in front. In performing it the carriage of the front rank executes an about at once, and moves to the place which was occupied by the other carriage. The latter follows the track of the former, executes the about on the same ground, and takes its place.

Note.—The tracks of the limber wheels are indicated by full lines, the track of the off-leader by broken lines.

FIGURE 27. There is but one kind of wheel, which is that with a moving pivot. The carriage on the pivot flank wheels in such a manner as to unmask the ground where the movement commenced. When the wheel is made with a section front, the pivot carriage describes a quadrant (*five* yards) of a circle whose radius is 3.25. With a battery front the pivot carriage describes a quadrant (*twenty-two* yards) of a circle whose radius is *fourteen*. If the wheel be ordered from a halt, the pivot carriage moves at a walk; if on the march, it preserves its gait. In all cases the marching wing regulates its gait in such a manner as to remain the shortest possible time in rear of the line, without urging the horses unnecessarily. In all wheels the guide is on the pivot flank, and the intervals are preserved from that flank. The chiefs of pieces act as guides, marching for that purpose with the leading carriages.

The *alignment* is made on the drivers of the wheel-horses, except in battery, when it is made on the hind wheels.

In giving commands the strength of the voice should be proportioned to the length of the line. When a chief of section does not hear the commands, he regulates his movement by what he sees executed by an adjoining chief. The command *Attention* is given by the captain at the commencement and at each renewal of the exercise; but afterward it is given only when he thinks it necessary to fix attention.

FORMATIONS OF THE BATTERY.

The three following orders constitute the different formations of the battery of manœuvre:

1. ORDER IN COLUMN. 2. ORDER IN LINE. 3. ORDER IN BATTERY.

ORDER IN COLUMN.

FIGURE 28. The *order in column* is that in which the battery is formed by sections; the carriages being in two files, and each piece being followed or preceded by its caisson.

The captain is generally *fourteen* yards from the column and opposite to its centre. But during the manœuvres he moves wherever his presence may be most necessary, and where his commands may be best heard.

Each chief of section is in line with his leading drivers, and midway between his leading carriages.

The chief of the line of caissons is in line with the captain, on the opposite side of the column, and *four* yards from it. But he does not change his position to conform to that of the captain.

Each chief of piece is on the left, and near the leading driver of his leading carriage.

The trumpeters are near the captain.

The guidon is habitually next the chief of the leading piece, or guide of the leading section, but takes post wherever the captain may direct.

ORDER IN LINE.

FIGURE 29. The *order in line* is that in which the carriages are formed in two lines: the horses all facing in the same direction, the pieces limbered, and each followed or preceded by its caisson.

The captain is generally *four* yards in front of the centre. But during the manœuvres he goes wherever his presence may be most necessary, and where his commands may be best heard.

Each chief of section is in line with his leading drivers, and midway between the leading carriages of his section.

The chief of the line of caissons is opposite the centre, *four* yards behind the rear line of carriages.

Each chief of piece is in the same position as in column.

The trumpeter, when he does not accompany the captain, is in line with the leading drivers, and *four* yards from the right flank.

The guidon is on the left of the trumpeter.

The interval between the carriages is *fourteen* yards.

The distance between the two lines is *two* yards.

The cannoneers are at their posts as in column.

Order in Battery.

Figure 30. The *order in battery* is that in which the pieces are prepared for firing: the pieces, limbers, and caissons being turned toward the enemy, and formed in three parallel lines.

The captain is generally on the left of the chief of the centre section; but he may go wherever his presence is required.

Each chief of section is habitually in the centre of his section, half-way between the lines of pieces and limbers.

The chief of the line of caissons is opposite the centre, *four* yards in rear of the line of caissons.

Each chief of piece is outside the file on the left of his piece, but near it, and opposite the middle of the trail handspike. During the real execution of the firings he habitually dismounts, and gives the reins of his horse to the driver of the wheel-horses of the limber, and takes his place on the right or left of the piece, in such position as will best enable him to observe the effect of the shot.

Each chief of caisson is on the left, and *four* yards in rear of the limber of the piece.

The trumpeters are near the captain. The guidon is on the flank of the line of caissons.

The interval between the pieces is *fourteen* yards.

The distance between the lines of pieces and limbers is *six* yards, measuring from the end of the handspike to the heads of the leading horses.

The distance between the lines of limbers and caissons is *eleven* yards, measuring from the rear of the limbers to the heads of the leading horses of the caissons.

The cannoneers are at their posts.

When the battery retires firing, the horses and drivers remain faced to the rear, after the first retrograde movement, that they may be ready to continue it.

Remarks on the Formations of the Battery.

During the manœuvres the captain is followed by the trumpeters, who must not leave him. On receiving an order from the captain for that purpose, they take the places assigned them in the order in line.

The guidon takes the place assigned him in the order *in column, in line,* or *in battery,* unless otherwise instructed by the captain, who directs him to take such position as he may think necessary.

The *double column* is a particular case of formation in column with a front of two pieces. It is formed on the centre section as head of the column; each of the other sections being in column of pieces in rear. When the battery contains four or eight pieces, the double column is formed upon the two central pieces as before.

Measures of the Elements Composing a Battery, and of its Formations.

The measures given in the three orders of the battery, and those which will be given hereafter, result from the dimensions of the different elements embraced. Those dimensions are given in the following table:

	Depth-yds.	Front-yds.
Pieces drawn by six horses	14	2
Caisson drawn by six horses	14	2
Limber drawn by six horses	11	2
Piece in battery with handspike	5	2
Column of sections	94	18
Line of battle	30	82
Line in battery	47	82
Section in line	30	18
Section in battery	47	18

Manning the Battery.

The gun-detachments and teams, having been properly told off, are marched to the park with the teams in front.

The chiefs of pieces and caissons, when mounted, march with the teams. The whole are conducted to the battery, the teams hitched, and detachments posted, as prescribed in the school of the section.

As soon as the teams are hitched and cannoneers posted, a minute inspection is made by the chiefs of pieces, who report to the chiefs of sections, and a similar inspection is made by the chiefs of sections, who report to the captain.

The officers, after reporting, will draw their sabres without waiting for a command to that effect. The chiefs of pieces will draw theirs on an intimation from the captain.

Article II.

Movements in Column.

To Unpark.

Everything being prepared for manœuvring, if the captain wishes to unpark by the right, he commands:

1. *By piece—from the right—front into column.*
2. March.

At the command March, the right piece, followed by its caisson, marches direct to the front, and the captain indicates the direction it should take. The other pieces and caissons follow the movement of the right piece, each so regulating its march by that which precedes it as to march in the same direction and *two* yards behind. Each chief of section directs the march of his carriages, which are so conducted by their chiefs as to enter the column by the most simple movement. The column of pieces is thus formed with a distance of *two* yards between the carriages.

The captain goes wherever his duty may require, but generally remains on the left flank, opposite the centre of the column.

The chief of the leading section places himself near the chief of the leading piece, and on his left; the other chiefs of sections *four* yards from the left flank, abreast the centres of their respective sections.

The chief of the line of caissons is opposite the centre of the column, and *four* yards from the right flank.

Each chief of piece and caisson, when mounted, is near his leading driver on the left.

The trumpeters are near the captain.

The guidon is near the chief of the leading piece, on his left.

When the battery is parked with the caissons in front, the captain causes it to unpark by the right by the same commands; the movements being executed in the same manner.

The battery may be unparked by the left according to the same principles, and by inverse means.

To Halt.

To halt the battery, when marching in column of pieces, the captain commands:

1. *Column.* 2. Halt.

At the second command, repeated by the chiefs of sections, all the carriages are immediately halted.

Change of Gait.

The changes of gait, in column of pieces, are executed by the following commands from the captain:

To pass from the walk to a trot:

1. *Trot.* 2. March.

To pass from the trot to a walk:

1. *Walk.* 2. March.

At the first command, repeated by the chiefs of sections, all the drivers and others on horseback prepare to change the gait; and at the second, repeated in like manner, they pass at once to the gait indicated by the first command.

To Form Sections.

When the battery is marching at a walk in column of pieces, to form sections at the same gait by gaining ground to the left, the captain commands:

1. *Form sections—left oblique.*   2. MARCH.   3. *Guide right.*

FIGURE 31. The chief of the leading section commands *Form section—left oblique*—MARCH—*Guide right* in succession after the captain.

At the command MARCH, the first two carriages, piece and caisson, advance *five* yards and halt. The two rear carriages oblique to the left, gain their intervals of *fourteen* yards, then move forward and place themselves abreast and on a line with the other two, dressing to the right.

The chief of the section takes his place midway between the leading carriages, and on a line with the lead drivers.

The other sections continue to march in column of pieces, and are formed successively by their chiefs; each commanding *Form section—left oblique* in time to command MARCH when the leading carriage of his section has arrived within *five* yards of its distance. The chief of section then commands: *Guide right.*

When the column of pieces is marching at a trot, the formation is executed according to the same principles and by the same commands. But the leading carriages, instead of advancing *five* yards and halting as before, pass to a walk as soon as the command MARCH is repeated by the chief of section. The other sections continue to march at a trot, and execute the movement at that gait, the two leading carriages of each section passing to a walk at the command MARCH, which must be given when they have closed to their proper distance.

When the column of pieces is at a halt, the formation is executed as prescribed for the column at a walk. In this case the carriages all move at the command MARCH, and the leading ones halt after advancing *five* yards.

When the column of pieces is marching at a walk, to form sections at a trot, gaining ground to the left, the captain commands:

    1. *Form sections—left oblique—trot.* 2. MARCH. 3. *Guide right.*

The chief of the leading section repeats the commands *Form section—left oblique—trot—* MARCH *— Guide right* in succession after the captain.

At the first command the chiefs of the other sections command *Trot;* and at the second, which they repeat, their sections commence the trot.

The chiefs of the second and third sections command *Form section—left oblique* in time to command MARCH when the leading carriage of each section has nearly gained its distance. The leading carriage then resumes the walk, and the chief of section commands *Guide right.*

The chiefs of sections superintend their carriages, and take the posts assigned them in the order in column as soon as their sections are formed.

Sections are formed by gaining ground to the right according to the same principles, and by inverse means. The commands are: *Form sections — right oblique —* MARCH *— Guide left;* or *Form sections—right oblique—trot—*MARCH*—Guide left.*

SCHOOL OF THE BATTERY.

THE BATTERY BEING IN COLUMN OF PIECES, TO FORM THE CAISSONS ON THE FLANK.

When the battery is in column of pieces with the caissons in rear, to form the pieces and caissons into separate columns, as in the flank march of a battery in line, the captain commands:

1. *Caissons left* (or *Caissons left—trot*). 2. MARCH. 3. *Guide right*.

These commands are repeated by the chiefs of sections, the caissons oblique at once to the left, gain the interval of *fourteen* yards, and place themselves opposite their pieces; the pieces closing upon each other at the same time to the usual distance. The gait is regulated as in the formation of sections; and when the movement is performed at a walk, the leading carriage halts after advancing its own length.

The chiefs of sections take their places as in column of sections.

The caissons are formed on the right according to the same principles, and by inverse means.

When the pieces are in rear, they are formed on the right or left of their caissons in the same manner, and by corresponding commands.

TO MARCH IN COLUMN.

The battery being in column at a halt, to advance, the captain commands:

1. *Column—forward*. 2. MARCH. 3. *Guide left* (or *right*).

The commands *forward*— MARCH — *Guide left* (or *right*) are repeated by the chiefs of sections. At the command MARCH, all the carriages advance, the guide maintains the direction, and the carriages, as well as the detachments of horse cannoneers, preserve their intervals and distances.

To Halt the Column.

The captain commands:

1. *Column.* 2. HALT.

At the first command the driver gathers his horses; at the second he halts.

To resume the march in column, the commands are:

1. *Column forward.* 2. MARCH.

To Change the Gait.

To trot, the captain commands:

1. *Trot.* 2. MARCH.

At the first command the driver gathers his horses. At the command MARCH, he takes the trot gradually, using for the near horse the legs and bridle hand, at the same time advancing the coupling rein with the right hand. If the off-horse does not obey this, the whip may be threatened, and, if necessary, used. When the horse obeys, replace the hand.

At the command *Trot out*—MARCH, the horses are urged to a rapid trot, and the gait maintained if necessary by the whip and spur.

At the command *Gallop*—MARCH, they are urged to the gallop, which gait is maintained until ordered to be changed.

To pass from the gallop to the trot, the commands are:

Trot—MARCH.

To pass from the *trot out* to the *trot*, the commands are:

Slow trot—MARCH.

To pass to a *walk*, the commands are:

Walk—MARCH.

To move at the rapid gaits from a halt, the commands *Trot*, etc., should be added to the first commands, so as to immediately precede those of execution. All *changes* of gait should be made gradually.

TO MARCH BY A FLANK.

The battery being in column, in march, or at a halt, to gain ground to the left, the captain commands:

1. *Column—by the left flank.* 2. MARCH.

FIGURE 32. The commands *By the left flank*—MARCH are repeated by the chiefs of sections. At the command MARCH, each carriage wheels at once to the left, and, when the wheel is pretty nearly completed, the captain commands:

1. FORWARD. 2. *Guide right.*

These commands are repeated by the chiefs of sections. At the command FORWARD, all the carriages march direct to the front.

The line is regularly established, and the carriages aligned in each rank, with their distances of *two* and intervals of *fourteen* yards. The chiefs of sections take their places between the leading carriages as in line.

To cause the battery to resume its original direction, the captain commands:

1. *Battery — by the right flank.* 2. MARCH. 3. FORWARD. 4. *Guide left.*

The commands *By the right flank* — MARCH — FORWARD — *Guide left* are repeated and executed according to the principles before described.

After the flank march, to march the battery in a direction opposite to the original one, the captain commands:

1. *Battery—by the left flank.* 2. MARCH. 3. FORWARD. 4. *Guide right.*

OBLIQUE MARCH.

The battery being in column, in march, or at a halt, to cause it to march obliquely, to gain ground to the front and left, the captain commands:

1. *Column—left oblique.* 2. MARCH.

FIGURE 33. The chiefs of sections repeat the commands *Left oblique*—MARCH after the captain.

At the command MARCH, all the carriages oblique at once to the left, and march in the new direction, moving in parallel lines, and preserving their intervals.

In obliquing, the heads of the horses in each rank are on a line parallel to the original front. The interval is *fourteen* yards, measured parallel to the front, and *ten* yards if measured on a line perpendicular to the oblique direction. In mounted batteries, each carriage of the right file marches in the prolongation of the left carriage of the rank which precedes its own, and at a distance of *nine* yards.

The chief of section conforms his movements to those of the section, and preserves his relative position.

The guide of the leading section is the guide of the column.

The officers conform to the movement, and preserve their relative positions.

To resume the original direction, the captain commands:

FORWARD.

This command is repeated by the chiefs of sections, and the carriages resume the original direction by obliquing to the right.

If the captain wishes to halt the column for the purpose of rectifying its alignments, intervals, or obliquity, he commands:

1. *Column.* 2. HALT.

And to resume the march in the oblique direction:

1. *Column.* 2. MARCH.

The commands HALT—MARCH are repeated by the chiefs of sections.

PASSAGE OF CARRIAGES IN COLUMN.

When the battery is marching in column, to change the relative positions of the front and rear ranks, without altering the gait, the captain commands:

1. *Pieces, pass your caissons* (or *Caissons, pass your pieces*). 2. MARCH.

These commands are repeated by the chiefs of sections; and at the command MARCH, the leading carriage of each piece halts. The rear carriage inclines to the right, passes it, takes the proper distance in front by inclining to the left, and halts. The chief of the piece joins it as it passes. To continue the march without halting the carriages which have passed, the instructor commands FORWARD when the passage is nearly completed.

To continue the march without halting the carriages of the rear rank, the captain commands: FORWARD when the passage is nearly completed, and the command is repeated by the chiefs of section.

When the column is marching at a trot, the passage is executed according to the same principles, and by the same commands, except that the carriages of the front rank move at a walk instead of halting at the command MARCH. The carriages of the rear rank execute the passage at a trot, and then change the gait to a walk.

When the column is at a halt, the passage is executed according to the same principles, and by the same commands. If the captain wishes to put the column in march immediately after the movement, he commands: FORWARD when the passage is about being completed, and then *Guide left* (or *right*). These commands are repeated by the chiefs of sections.

When the column is marching at a walk, to execute the passage at a trot, the captain commands:

1. *Pieces, pass your caissons* — trot (or *Caissons, pass your pieces—trot*). 2. MARCH.

These commands are repeated by the chiefs of sections. At the command MARCH the carriages of the front rank in each section continue to march at a walk. Those of the rear rank execute the passage at a trot, and resume the walk as soon as the passage is completed.

ABOUT IN COLUMN.

The battery being in column, in march, or at a halt, to face it to the rear, the captain commands:

1. *Pieces and caissons—left about.* 2. MARCH.

These commands are repeated by the chiefs of sections; and at the second all the carriages execute the about. When the movement is about being completed, the captain commands: *Column* — HALT; or FORWARD—*Guide right* (or *left*): the commands HALT, or FORWARD—*Guide right* (or *left*) are repeated by the chiefs of sections.

COUNTERMARCH IN COLUMN.

The battery being in column, in march, or at a halt, to execute the countermarch in each section, the captain commands:

    1. *Countermarch.* 2. MARCH.

These commands are repeated by the chiefs of sections, and at the second each piece and its caisson execute the countermarch. When the movement is about being completed, the captain commands: *Column*—HALT; or FORWARD—*Guide right* (or *left*).

These commands are repeated as in the preceding paragraph.

TO CHANGE DIRECTION IN COLUMN.

The battery being in column, in march, or at a halt, to cause it to change direction to the left, the captain commands:

    Head of column to the left.

FIGURE 34. The chief of the leading section commands: *Left wheel* — MARCH; and afterward FORWARD.

At the command MARCH, the pivot carriage executes the wheel without changing the gait, the carriage on the wheeling flank wheels in such manner as to conform to its movements, increasing the gait, and preserving the intervals. At the command FORWARD, which is given as soon as it is in the new direction, the pivot carriage moves direct to the front; the other resumes its original gait after completing the wheel and arriving upon the same line. The carriages of the rear rank preserve their distances, and follow those of the front rank.

Each of the other sections, on arriving at the point where the first wheeled, executes the same movement, and by the same commands from its chief.

Each chief of section must give the command *Left wheel* in time to command MARCH when the heads of his leaders are *three and a quarter* yards from the wheeling point. And the command FORWARD must be given as soon as the leading pivot carriage has entered the new direction.

The change of direction to the right is executed according to the same principles, and by inverse means.

An oblique change of direction is executed according to the same principles by the command:

Head of column—left (or *right*) *half-wheel.*

The chiefs of sections command successively: *Left* (or *right*) *half-wheel* — MARCH — FORWARD; the command FORWARD being given, in this case, when the leading pivot carriage of each section is about finishing the left or right oblique.

TO DIMINISH THE FRONT OF A COLUMN ON THE MARCH.

The battery marching at a walk in column of sections, to form column of pieces from the right, at that gait, the captain commands:

1. *By the right—break sections.* 2. MARCH.

Figure 35. The chief of the leading section commands successively after the captain:

*By the right—break section—*March.

At the command March, the right carriages continue to move forward at a walk, the left carriages obliquing to enter the column in their rear.

The other sections are broken in succession by the same commands from their chiefs; the command March being given when the wheel-horses of the left carriages of the next preceding section enter the right oblique.

The battery marching at a walk in column of sections, to form column of pieces from the right at a trot, the captain commands:

1. *By the right—break sections—trot.* 2. March.

The chief of the leading section commands successively after the captain: *By the right—break section—trot—*March; and the right carriages of the leading section move forward at a moderate trot. The left carriages of the same section commence the trot on obliquing to enter the column.

The other sections are broken successively by the same commands from their chiefs; and the carriages are regulated by each other, as in breaking sections at a walk.

This formation is executed from the left according to the same principles, and by inverse means.

In Column with the Caissons on the Flank, to Replace them in Front or Rear.

The battery being in column, with the caissons on the flank, to re-establish them in rear of their pieces, the captain commands:

1. *Caissons, rear* (or *Caissons, rear—trot*). 2. March.

Each chief of section repeats the commands in time to command March when the leading piece of his section is to commence the movement.

At the command March, the piece at the head of the column moves forward at the required gait, and its caisson places itself in rear by an oblique. The other pieces move forward in succession, and are followed by their caissons in like manner.

All the carriages preserve the usual distances in column.

This movement is performed at the different gaits, and according to the principles prescribed for breaking sections.

To place the caissons in front of their pieces, the commands are:

1. *Caissons, front* (or *Caissons, front—trot*). 2. March.

The caissons oblique successively, and take their positions at *two* yards distance in front of their pieces, which then follow their movements.

To Form the Park.

The battery being in column of pieces, and near the ground on which it is to be parked, will be formed by one of the following commands:

1. *At—yards interval.* { *Forward into park—right* (or *left*) *oblique.*
  To the right (or *left*) *into park.*
  On the right (or *left*) *into park.* }
2 March.

To form forward into park. The column approaches the park from the rear, the leading piece being in rear of the ground on which it is to rest.

At the command MARCH, the leading piece marches direct to the front, and halts at its proper place; all the other carriages oblique to the right (or left) until near their places in park, when they change direction to the front so as to come up square on the line. They halt a little in rear of the line, and dress forward on the carriage already established.

To form to the right into park. The captain, approaching the park by its right, directs the column parallel to the front and *forty* yards behind it. At the command MARCH, which is given when the leading piece is *three* yards from the point opposite the position which it is to occupy, the chief of section wheels it to the right, moves it forward, and halts it at its position. The other carriages move straight forward; each one wheels to the right when *three* yards from the point opposite to the position it is to occupy in park, marches forward, and places itself on the right of and in line with those already established.

To form to the left into park is executed according to the same principles, and by inverse means.

To form on the right into park. The captain, approaching the park by its right, directs the column parallel to the front and *forty* yards in rear.

The leading piece is wheeled to the right and established in its position as before; the next, passing in rear of it, places itself in line on its left in like manner, and so with the others.

When the park consists of two or more lines, the same principles are observed; each carriage of the rear ranks follows its file-leader in its movements.

The park should be formed on the left according to the same principles, and by inverse means.

Each chief of section directs the march of carriages,

and each carriage is conducted to its place in park by its particular chief. When the nature of the ground requires, the detachments are ordered to leave their pieces successively when they are about to enter the park.

Article III.

To Pass from the Order in Column to the Order in Line, and the Reverse.

In all formations in line or column the movements are the same, whether the pieces or caissons lead.

Forward into Line.

The battery being in column at a halt, to form it into line on the head of the column, gaining ground to the left, the captain commands:

1. *Forward into line—left oblique.* 2. March. 3. *Guide right.* 4. Front.

Figure 36. At the first command the chief of the leading section commands: *Section—forward*, and those of the other sections: *Section—left oblique*. At the command March, repeated by the chiefs of sections, the leading section moves to the front, and its chief repeats the command for the guide. After advancing *eighteen* yards he commands: *Section—Halt—Right* Dress.

Each of the other chiefs of sections repeats the commands for the guide, and conducts his section by a left oblique, until by the direct march it may gain its proper interval from the section immediately on its right He then commands: Forward, and when within four yards of the line, *Section*—HALT—*Right* DRESS.

When the battery is aligned, the captain commands: FRONT.

The movement is executed on the opposite flank according to the same principles, and by inverse means.

In this case the commands are: *Forward into line—right oblique*—MARCH—*Guide left*—FRONT.

The formation forward into line, by a right or left oblique, is executed in a similar manner when the column is in march. In this case the chief of the leading section gives no command except for the guide, until he has advanced the distance before prescribed. He then halts his section as before.

TO FORM LINE FACED TO THE REAR.

The battery being in column at a halt, to form it into line faced to the rear, on the head of the column gaining ground to the left, the captain commands:

1. *Into line faced to the rear—left oblique.* 2. MARCH. 3. *Guide right.* 4. FRONT.

FIGURE 37. At the first command the chief of the leading section commands: *Section — forward;* and those of the other sections: *Section—left oblique.* At the command MARCH, repeated by the chiefs of sections, the movement is executed as prescribed for the preceding movement, with the exception of the alignment. When the leading section has advanced *eighteen* yards, it is halted by its chief until the centre section arrives upon the same line. He then commands: *Countermarch*—MARCH; and when the countermarch is nearly completed: *Section*—HALT—*Left* DRESS.

The centre section is halted upon the line in like manner until the left section comes up, and is then countermarched and aligned by the same commands.

When the left section arrives upon the line, it is countermarched before halting, and then aligned like the rest.

When the centre and left sections are countermarched, the commands HALT — *Left* DRESS should be given, if possible, when they are *four* yards in rear of the line on which the leading section is established.

When the battery is aligned, the captain commands: FRONT.

The movement is executed on the opposite flank according to the same principles, and by inverse means. In this case the commands are: *Into line faced to the rear—right oblique*—MARCH—*Guide left*—FRONT.

The formation into line faced to the rear, by a right or left oblique, is executed in a similar manner when the column is in march. In this case, as the leading section is already in motion, its chief only repeats the command for the guide.

The countermarch of sections will be executed at the gait ordered for the rear of the column.

TO FORM LINE TO THE RIGHT OR LEFT.

The battery being in column, in march, or in halt, to form it into line to the left, the captain commands:

1. *Left into line, wheel.* 2. MARCH. 3. *Battery*—HALT.
4. *Left* DRESS. 5. FRONT.

FIGURE 38. At the first command the chiefs of sections command: *Section—Left wheel;* and at the second, which they repeat, all the sections wheel to the left. Each chief of section commands: *Forward—*

Guide left as soon as his leading pivot carriage has taken the new direction.

When the rear carriages have completed the wheel, and the sections are in line, the captain commands: *Battery*—HALT—*Left* DRESS.

The commands HALT—*Left* DRESS, are repeated by the chiefs of sections, and, when the alignment is completed, the captain commands: FRONT.

The battery is formed into line to the right according to the same principles, and by inverse means.

To Form Line on the Right or Left.

The battery marching in column, to form it into line on the right, the captain commands:

1. *On the right into line.* 2. MARCH. 3. *Guide right.* 4. FRONT.

FIGURE 39. At the first command the chief of the leading section commands: *Section—right wheel;* and at the second, which he repeats, the section wheels to the right. As soon as the leading pivot carriage enters the new direction, he commands: FORWARD—*Guide right;* and as the section completes the wheel and unmasks the column, he commands: *Section—*HALT—*Right* DRESS.

The chiefs of the other sections repeat the command for the guide, and their sections continue to move forward. As each section passes the one preceding it in the formation, its chief establishes it on the line, with the proper interval, by the same commands. The commands *Section*—HALT—*Right* DRESS are given when the section is *four* yards in rear of the line.

When the battery is aligned, the captain commands: FRONT.

The line is formed on the left according to the same principles, and by inverse means. The commands are: *On the left into line*—MARCH—*Guide left*—FRONT.

When the column is at a halt, the line is formed on the right or left in the same manner. In this case the chiefs of the two rear sections command: *Section —forward*, and afterward repeat the commands MARCH—*Guide right* (or *left*).

TO BREAK INTO COLUMN TO THE FRONT.

The battery being in a line at a halt, to break into the column to the front from the right, the captain commands:

1. *By section from the right—front into column.*
2. MARCH. 3. *Guide left.*

FIGURE 40. At the first command the chief of the right section commands: *Section—forward;* and those of the other sections: *Section—right oblique.* At the command MARCH, repeated by the chief of the right section, that section moves forward, and its chief repeats the command for the guide.

Each of the other chiefs of sections repeats the commands MARCH—*Guide left* after the section on his right has commenced the movement, and when the leaders of its rear carriages are in line with him. After obliquing sufficiently to gain the rear of the preceding section, he commands: FORWARD.

To commence the movement at a trot, the captain commands:

1. *By section from the right—front into column—trot.*
2. MARCH. 3. *Guide left.*

At the first command the chief of the right section commands: *Section—forward trot;* those of the other sections: *Section—forward.* At the command MARCH, repeated by the chiefs of sections, the right section moves at a trot, and the other sections at a walk, their chiefs adding the commands for the guide.

The chiefs of the centre and left sections command: *Section—right oblique—trot* in time to command MARCH when the leaders of the rear carriages of the section on their right are opposite to them.

This rule for commencing movements at a trot is general.

The movement is executed from the left according to the same principles, and by inverse means.

TO BREAK INTO COLUMN TO THE REAR.

The battery being in line, in march, or at a halt, to break into column to the rear from one of the flanks, the captain executes an about or a countermarch, according to the kind of carriage he may wish in front, then halts the battery, and breaks it into column to the front by the preceding manœuvre.

TO BREAK INTO COLUMN TO THE RIGHT OR LEFT.

The battery being in line, in march, or at a halt, to break it into column to the left, the captain commands:

1. *By section—left wheel.* 2. MARCH. 3. FORWARD. 4. *Guide left.*

FIGURE 41. At the first command the chiefs of sections command: *Section—left wheel;* and at the second, repeated by those chiefs, all the sections wheel to the left. When the wheels are nearly completed, the captain commands: FORWARD—*Guide left;* and the chiefs of sections repeat the commands.

When the column is not to advance, the command *Column*—HALT is substituted for FORWARD—*Guide left.*

The battery is broken into column to the right according to the same principles, and by inverse means.

TO BREAK INTO COLUMN TO THE FRONT FROM ONE FLANK TO MARCH TOWARD THE OTHER.

The battery being in line at a halt, to break from the right to march to the left, the captain commands:

1. *By section—break from the right—to march to the left.* 2. MARCH. 3. *Guide left.*

FIGURE 42. At the first command the chief of the right section commands: *Section—forward;* and at the second, which he repeats, the section moves forward, and he commands: *Guide left.* After advancing *eleven* yards, he changes the direction to the left by the commands: *Section—left wheel*—MARCH—FORWARD.

Each of the other chiefs of sections commands: *Section—forward* in time to command MARCH when the limber wheels of the rear carriages in the section preceding his own arrive in front of him. He then conducts the section to the front, changes its direction to the left, and places it in rear of the preceding section by the commands already prescribed for the section on the right.

The battery is broken from the left to march to the right according to the same principles, and by inverse means.

To Break into Column to the Rear from One Flank to March toward the Other.

The battery being in line at a halt, to break to the rear from one flank to march toward the other, the captain first executes an about or countermarch, according to the kind of carriage he may wish in front. He then halts the battery, and executes the preceding manœuvre.

To Break into Column to the Front when the Battery is Marching in Line.

The battery marching in line at a walk, to break into column to the front from the right, and at the same gait, the captain commands:

1. *By the right — break into sections.* 2. March. 3. *Guide left.*

The chief of the right section repeats the command for the guide, and his section continues to move at the same gait. At the command MARCH, the other sections are halted by the command *Section* — HALT from their chiefs.

The halted sections are put in motion successively by their chiefs; each commanding *Section — right oblique* in time to command MARCH when the leaders of the rear carriages in the section on his right arrive opposite to him.

When the battery is marching at a trot, the movement is executed according to the same principles. But the sections which halted in the preceding case slacken the gait to a walk at the commands *Walk*— MARCH from their chiefs. They again trot, and enter the column by the commands *Section — right oblique — trot* — MARCH — FORWARD.

When the battery is marching in line at a walk, to break into column from the right at a trot, the captain commands:

1. *By the right — break into sections — trot.* 2. MARCH.
3. *Guide left.*

At the first command the chief of the right section commands: *Trot;* and at the second, which he repeats, the section changes its gait to a trot. He afterward repeats the command *Guide left.*

Each of the other sections continues to march at a walk until required to enter the column, when its chief conducts it, as already described, by the commands *Section — right oblique — trot —* MARCH — FORWARD.

The battery is broken into column from the left according to the same principles, and by inverse means.

TO FORM LINE ADVANCING.

When the battery is marching in column at a walk, to form it into line at a trot, gaining ground to the left, and continue the march, the captain commands:

1. *Form line advancing — left oblique — trot.* 2. MARCH.
3. *Guide right.*

The chief of the leading section repeats the command for the guide, and his section continues to move at a walk.

At the first command the chiefs of the other sections command: *Section — left oblique — trot.* The command MARCH is repeated by the same chiefs; and when the oblique movement is commenced, they repeat the command *Guide right.* Each chief commands: FORWARD as soon as his section has obliqued sufficiently to the left, and *Walk* in time to command **March** as it arrives on the line.

When the battery is marching in column at a trot, the movement is executed according to the same principles. In this case the captain does not command *Trot;* and the chief of the leading section commands: *Walk*—**March** successively after the first and second commands of the captain. The chiefs of the other sections give the same commands as their sections arrive on the line.

The movement is executed so as to gain ground to the right according to the same principles, and by inverse means.

To Form Double Column on the Centre Section.

The battery being in line at a halt, to form double column on the centre section, the captain commands:

1. *Double column on the centre.* 2. **March.** 3. *Guide right (or left).*

Figure 43. At the first command the chief of the centre section commands: *Section—forward;* the chief of the right section: *Section—left oblique;* and the chief of the left section: *Section—right oblique.* At the command **March**, repeated by the chief of the centre section, that section marches to the front, and its chief repeats the command for the guide.

When the wheel-horses in the rear rank of the centre section have passed the leaders in the front rank of the other sections, the chiefs of those sections repeat the command **March**, and the sections commence the oblique.

When the piece nearest the column is about entering it, in each of these sections, the chief of the right section commands: *By the left—break section*—MARCH; and the chief of the left: *By the right—break section*—MARCH. The right and left sections, without change of gait, then form into columns of pieces in rear of the right and left carriages of the centre section.

The chiefs of the flank sections are careful to make their pieces enter the column at the proper time. When the column is formed, they place themselves *four yards* outside of it, the one highest in rank opposite the leaders of his leading carriage, the other opposite the leaders of the front carriage of his rear piece. In these positions they command the pieces abreast of them as sections for the time being.

The chief of the line of caissons follows the movement, sees that his carriages do not enter the column too soon, and, when the column is formed, places himself *four* yards in rear of its centre.

When the battery is marching at a walk, to form the double column at the same gait, the captain commands:

1. *Double column on the centre.* 2. MARCH. 3. *Guide right* (or *left*).

The chief of the centre section repeats the command for the guide, and the section continues to advance.

At the command MARCH, the other sections are halted by the command *Section*—HALT from their chiefs. They are afterward formed into column by the commands and means prescribed for forming double column from a halt.

When the battery is marching at a trot, the double column is formed according to the same principles. In this case the flank sections pass to a walk, instead of halting as before, and resume the trot, to oblique and enter the column. The commands from their chiefs are: *Walk* — MARCH — *Section* — *left* (or *right*) *oblique*—*trot*—MARCH, and *By the left* (or *right*)—*break section*—MARCH.

When the battery is marching at a walk, to form the double column at a trot, the captain commands:

1. *Double column on the centre*—*trot*. 2. MARCH. 3. *Guide right* (or *left*).

At the first command the chief of the centre section commands: *Trot*. At the second, which he repeats, the section moves forward at a moderate trot, and he repeats the command for the guide.

The flank sections continue to walk until the centre has advanced sufficiently to allow them to oblique, and are then formed into column as already prescribed; their chiefs commanding: *Section*—*left* (or *right*) *oblique*—*trot*—MARCH; and *By the left* (or *right*) —*break section*—MARCH.

If the battery is at a halt, the chief of the centre section commands: *Forward*—*trot;* and the chiefs of the other sections: *Forward* after the first command from the captain. At the second, repeated by the chiefs of sections, all move forward, the flank sections at a walk; and the movement is completed as already directed.

To form the double column with a battery of four or of eight pieces, the captain gives the same commands as with a battery of six. In the four-gun battery, the right section is broken into column of pieces by the left, and the left section is broken by the right at the commands of the chiefs of sections, who place themselves on the outer flanks of the column, and command the temporary sections, as directed for the flank sections of the battery of six pieces.

In the battery of eight pieces, the double column is formed on the two centre pieces according to the same principles. The flank sections oblique, and form in column of pieces behind the centre sections at the commands of their chiefs, who then take post on the flanks of the column, and command the temporary sections formed from their own, the senior of the two commanding the leading one.

To Deploy the Double Column into Line to the Front.

The battery being in double column at a halt, to form it into line to the front, the captain commands:

1. *Forward into line.* 2. March. 3. Front.

Figure 44. At the first command the chief of the centre section commands: *Section—forward;* the chief of the right section: *Section into line—right oblique;* and the chief of the left section: *Section into line—left oblique.* At the command March, repeated by these chiefs, the centre section advances *five* yards, and its chief commands: *Section—*Halt*—Right* (or *left,* Dress.

The flank sections oblique to the right and left; and as their pieces arrive in rear of their proper places on the line, they move forward, halt, and dress toward the centre without command.

As soon as the battery is aligned, the captain commands: Front.

When the column is marching, the movement is executed in the same manner. In this case the chief of the centre section does not command *Section—*

forward—MARCH; but halts and aligns his section after advancing *five* yards.

When the column is marching at a trot, to deploy it into line to the front at the same gait, without discontinuing the march, the captain commands:

1. *Form line advancing.* 2. MARCH. 3. *Guide right* (or *left*).

At the first command the chief of the centre section commands: *Walk;* the chief of the right section: *Section into line—right oblique;* and the chief of the left section: *Section into line—left oblique.* At the command MARCH, repeated by these chiefs, the centre section slackens its gait to a walk, and the flank sections deploy. As each piece arrives upon the line its gait is changed to a walk without command. The movement is executed as in the preceding cases; but when the line is formed it continues to advance, the captain commanding *Guide right* (or *left*), which command is repeated by the chiefs of sections.

When the column is marching at a walk, to deploy it into line to the front at a trot, without discontinuing the march, the captain commands:

1. *Form line advancing—trot.* 2. MARCH. 3. *Guide right* (or *left*).

At the first command the chief of the right section commands: *Section into line—right oblique—trot;* and the chief of the left section: *Section into line—left oblique—trot.* At the command MARCH, repeated by these chiefs, the flank sections deploy at a trot; the centre section continues to march at a walk; and, the line having been formed as in the preceding case, the captain gives the command for the guide.

When the battery consists of four or eight pieces, the double column is deployed into line to the front by the same commands from the captain as when it consists of six. The chiefs of sections give the same commands as in the other case. When the line is to be halted, as in forming *forward into line*, the leading chief commands: HALT—*Right* (or *left*) DRESS as soon as the leading carriages have advanced *five* yards; and the alignment is made upon the central carriages.

TO FORM THE DOUBLE COLUMN INTO LINE TO THE RIGHT OR LEFT.

The battery being in double column at a halt, to form it into line to the right, the captain commands:

1. *To and on the right into line.* 2. MARCH. 3. FRONT.

At the first command the chief of the leading section commands: *Section—Right wheel;* and the other chiefs of sections: *Forward.* At the second, repeated by those chiefs, the leading section wheels to the right, and is established on the line. The other pieces advance under the direction of their chiefs and of the chiefs of sections, wheel to the right in succession as they arrive opposite their places, establish themselves on the line, and dress upon the pieces already aligned. When the alignment is completed, the captain commands: FRONT.

When the column is marching, the line is formed to the right in the same manner, except that the chiefs of the flank sections omit the commands *Forward — March.* The line is formed to the left according to the same principles, and by inverse means.

When the battery consists of four or eight pieces, the double column is deployed into line to the right or left by the same commands from the captain as when it consists of six. In this case the leading pieces are wheeled to the right or left, as a section, and established on the line. For this purpose the leading chief of section commands: *Right* (or *left*) *wheel*—MARCH—FORWARD—*Guide right* (or *left*)—HALT—*Right* (or *left*) DRESS. The other pieces move forward, wheel in succession as they arrive opposite their places, and form on the line, as already described.

ARTICLE IV.

MOVEMENTS IN LINE.

TO ADVANCE IN LINE.

The battery being in line at a halt, to cause it to advance, the captain indicates to the guide the points on which he is to march, and commands:

1. *Battery—forward.* 2. MARCH. 3. *Guide right* (or *left*).

The commands *Forward*—MARCH—*Guide right* (or *left*) are repeated by the chiefs of sections. At the command MARCH, all the carriages move forward at a walk, and the chiefs of sections preserve the alignment toward that chief of carriage who serves as *guide of the line.* The guide marches steadily in the given direction, and the chiefs of carriages regulate their intervals and alignment by him.

The carriages of the rear rank follow those in front at their appropriate distance of *two* yards. The chief of the line of caissons superintends the march of the rear rank of carriages, and moves wherever his presence may be necessary for that purpose.

To Halt the Battery and Align it.

When the battery is marching in line, to halt and align it, the captain commands:

1. *Battery*—Halt. 2. *Right* (or *left*) Dress. 3. Front.

The commands Halt—*Right* (or *left*) Dress are repeated by the chiefs of sections. At the first command the carriages and detachments halt, and at the second align themselves by the right (or left) in their respective ranks; the carriages dressing by the drivers of their wheel-horses. The carriages are placed as squarely on the line as possible, without opening or closing the intervals. The captain superintends the alignment of the front rank of carriages, and the chief of the line of caissons that of the rear; each placing himself for that purpose on the flank of the guide. When the battery is aligned, the captain commands: Front.

When the battery is halted, if it cannot be aligned by slight movements, the captain causes one or two carriages from one of the flanks or centre to advance *four* yards, or to a greater distance if necessary, and then causes the alignment to be made by the right, left, or centre, by the command *Right, Left,* or *On the centre*—Dress. At this command the carriages and detachments move forward, and align themselves according to the principles just explained; the drivers halting a little in rear of the line, and dressing forward, so as to place the carriages as squarely upon it as possible.

Changes of Gait.

When the battery is marching in line, the changes of gait are effected by the commands and means prescribed for changes when marching in column.

To March by a Flank.

Figure 45. The battery being in line, in march or at a halt, to cause it to move in the direction of one of its flanks, the captain commands:

1. *Battery—by the right* (or *left*) *flank.* 2. March.

And the movement is executed as prescribed for the same movement when the battery is marching in column.

Oblique March.

Figure 46. The battery being in line, in march or at a halt, to gain ground to the front and toward one of the flanks, and afterward resume the direct march, the captain commands: *Battery—left* (or *right*) *oblique*, which is executed in the same manner as the oblique in column.

Passage of Carriages in Line.

When the battery is in line, the passage of carriages is executed by the commands and means prescribed for the passage of carriages in column.

About in Line.

When the battery is in line, the about is executed by the commands and means prescribed for the same movement when in column, substituting the word *battery* for *column*.

Countermarching in Line.

The countermarch of a battery in line is executed by the commands and means prescribed for the same movement in column, substituting the word *battery* for *column* in the command.

To Change Direction in Line.

The battery being in line at a halt, to wheel it to the right, the captain commands:

1. *Battery — right wheel.* 2. March. 3. Forward. 4. *Battery*—Halt. 5. *Right* Dress. 6. Front.

The commands *Right wheel*—March—Forward—Halt—*Right* Dress are repeated by the chiefs of sections.

Figure 47. At the command March, the pivot carriage moves at a walk, and describes a quadrant (*twenty-two* yards) of a circle whose radius is *fourteen* yards. The other carriages move at a trot, and preserve their intervals from the pivot. They regulate their gaits according to the distance from the pivot, so as to remain as short a time as possible in rear of the line, without urging their horses injuriously, and so as to arrive upon it in succession. The carriages of the rear rank follow at the proper distance in the tracks of those in front.

At the command Forward, which is given when the leading pivot carriage has described its arc of *twenty-two* yards, the carriage moves direct to the front; and when the rear pivot carriage is in the new direction, the captain commands: *Battery*—Halt—*Right* Dress. The commands Forward — Halt — *Right* Dress are repeated by the chiefs of the right section immediately after the captain, and by the other chiefs in time to be applicable to their sections; the pivot carriages halting at the command HALT, and the others halting and dressing toward the pivot as they arrive in succession on the line.

When the battery is aligned, the captain commands: FRONT.

The battery is wheeled to the left according to the same principles, and by inverse means.

When the battery is at a halt or marching in line, to wheel it to the right and continue the march, the captain commands:

1. *Battery—right wheel.* 2. MARCH. 3. FORWARD.

The movement is executed as already described, except that the pivot carriage, after wheeling, continues to march in the new direction, and the others conform to its gait and direction as they arrive on the line.

The direction is changed on the left according to the same principles, and by inverse means.

TO CLOSE INTERVALS IN LINE.

When the battery is marching in line at a walk or trot, to diminish its intervals, the captain commands:

1. *On right* (or *left*) *piece of ——— section to ——— yards—close intervals.*

FIGURE 48. The chief of the section designated repeats the command: *On right* (or *left*) *piece to ——— yards—close intervals;* and the other chiefs of sections command: *Right* (or *left*) *to ——— yards—close intervals.* At the command MARCH, repeated by the same chiefs, the piece designated as the one of direction moves forward at a walk, and the others oblique toward it at a trot. Each obliquing carriage regulates its march by the one next toward the carriage of direction, and, after closing to the prescribed interval, moves forward on the alignment of the directing carriage, and slackens the gait to a walk.

As soon as the intervals are closed, the command for the guide is renewed by the captain, and repeated by the chiefs of sections.

When the intervals are to be closed toward one of the flanks, the captain commands:

1. *On right (or left) piece to ——— yards—close intervals.* 2. MARCH.

ABOUT OR COUNTERMARCH WITH DIMINISHED INTERVALS.

The battery being in line with diminished intervals, in march or at a halt, to execute an about or countermarch, the captain commands:

1. *Pieces and caissons — left about (or countermarch).*
2. *Right pieces forward (or right pieces forward — trot).*
3. MARCH.

The chiefs of sections repeat these commands. At the second the right carriages of each section move forward, and as soon as they are disengaged from the line, the captain commands: MARCH. All the carriages execute the required movement at this command, with the gait corresponding to that of the carriages in front.

In regard to the change of gait, these movements are executed according to the principles prescribed in order that the right carriages may move out of line and return to it again at the completion of the movement.

To Resume Intervals.

When the battery is marching in line with diminished intervals, to cause the regular intervals to be resumed, the captain commands:

1. *On right (or left) piece of ——— section—full intervals.* 2. March.

Figure 49. The chief of the section designated repeats the command: *On right (or left) piece—full intervals;* and the other chiefs of sections command: *From the right (or left)—full intervals.*

At the command March, repeated by the chiefs of sections, the carriage of direction in each rank continues to march to the front, and the others oblique from it at an increased gait, to regain their intervals. Each carriage regulates its march by the one adjoining toward the carriage of direction, and, when the interval is regained, moves forward on the alignment, and resumes its gait.

As soon as the movement is completed, the command for the guide is renewed by the captain, and repeated by the chiefs of sections.

When the intervals are to be resumed from one of the flanks, the captain commands:

1. *On right (or left) piece—full intervals.* 2. March.

Passage of Obstacles.

When the battery is marching in line, to pass an obstacle which presents itself in front of one of the sections, the captain commands:

1. ―――― *Section.* 2. Obstacle.

At the command Obstacle, the chief of the section designated observes the obstacle, and gives the necessary commands for closing on one of the adjoining sections, removing from it, breaking his section, or halting it, and forming in column in rear of one of the adjoining sections. The section generally resumes the regular march by means the inverse of those used for passing the obstacle. It resumes its place at an increased gait, and by the commands *Section into line*—March from its chief.

The passage of defiles is nothing more than the passage of obstacles, which requires the line to be broken into column of sections, by one of the manœuvres prescribed for passing from the order in line to the order in column. When it becomes necessary to break the sections, they should be formed again in succession by their chiefs as soon as the ground will permit.

Article V.

FORMATIONS IN BATTERY.

In Line, with Pieces in Front, to Form in Battery to the Front.

When the battery is in line at a halt, with the pieces in front, to form in battery to the front, the captain commands:

1. In battery. 2. *Guide left.* 3. March.

Figure 50. At the command In battery, the caissons stand fast and the pieces advance. The intervals and alignment are preserved, and the chiefs of pieces and of the section march at their places in line.

At the command MARCH, which is given as soon as they have advanced *seventeen* yards, the chiefs of pieces and of the section halt, and the pieces execute an about. As soon as the about is completed, the pieces are halted, unlimbered, and prepared for firing, the limbers being taken to their places in battery by an about.

When the pieces come about, the one already designated as such continues to be the guide, and the alignment is made on it.

When the cannoneers are marching by the sides of their pieces they halt at the command MARCH, allow their pieces to pass them, change sides, and move forward to the posts they are to occupy when their pieces have completed the about. They are not required to observe any particular order during this movement.

When the cannoneers are mounted on the ammunition-chests, those on the caissons dismount and run to their posts at the command IN BATTERY. Those on the pieces dismount after the about.

The chiefs of pieces, and of the section, take their posts *in battery* as soon as that formation is completed. *This rule is general.*

After the formation, the captain rectifies the alignment if necessary. The piece originally designated as such continues to be the guide until the movement is completed, and the alignment is made upon it.

When the battery is marching in line, with the pieces in front, it is formed in battery to the front according to the same principles, and by the commands:

1. IN BATTERY. 2. MARCH.

These commands are repeated by the chiefs of sections, and, at the command IN BATTERY, the caissons halt, the cannoneers dismounting and running to their posts.

TO FORM IN BATTERY TO THE FRONT, BY THROWING THE CAISSONS TO THE REAR.

When the battery is in line at a halt, with the pieces or caissons in front, to form in battery to the front by throwing the caissons to the rear, the captain commands:

ACTION FRONT.

This command is repeated by the chiefs of sections, and the pieces are unlimbered and wheeled about by hand. The limbers and caissons, reversing to the left at the same time, move to the rear, and take their places in battery at their proper distances by another reverse.

When the cannoneers are mounted on the ammunition-chests, they dismount as soon as the command ACTION FRONT is given, and run to their posts.

The battery is generally in line at a halt when this mode of coming into action is resorted to. It may also be used in successive formations by giving the command ACTION FRONT when a part of the battery has been halted on the line. But with bad ground or heavy pieces this mode of coming into action should not be used.

IN LINE, WITH CAISSONS IN FRONT, TO FORM IN BATTERY TO THE FRONT.

When the battery is in line at a halt, with the

caissons in front, to form in battery to the front, the captain commands:

1. *Pieces, pass your caissons*—MARCH. 2. IN BATTERY—*Guide left* (or *right*). 3. MARCH.

FIGURE 51. These commands are repeated by the chiefs of sections, the pieces pass their caissons, and, at the command IN BATTERY, given as soon as the pieces have passed their caissons, the formation is executed as prescribed for forming in battery with pieces in front.

When the battery is marching in line, with the caissons in front, it is formed in battery to the front according to the same principles, and by the commands *Pieces pass your caissons* (or *Pieces, pass your caissons—trot*)—MARCH—IN BATTERY—*Guide left*—MARCH.

IN LINE, WITH PIECES IN FRONT, TO FORM IN BATTERY TO THE REAR.

When the battery is in line at a halt, with the pieces in front, to form in battery to the rear, the captain commands:

1. *Fire to the rear.* 2. *Caissons, pass your pieces—trot*—MARCH. 3. IN BATTERY.

FIGURE 52. The commands are repeated by the chiefs of sections. At the second, the caissons oblique to the right, pass their pieces at a brisk trot, advance *seventeen* yards beyond them, execute a reverse together, and take their places in battery. At the third, which is given as soon as the caissons have passed, the cannoneers unlimber and prepare for firing.

When the cannoneers are mounted on the ammunition-chests the caissons halt to allow the cannoneers to dismount, before executing the reverse. As soon as the caissons halt, the cannoneers dismount and run to their posts. When the battery is at a halt, as in the present case, it is considered better to dismount the cannoneers before commencing the movement. The chief of the line of caissons precedes the movement of his carriages, and places himself on the line to be occupied by their leaders when the reverse is commenced. He takes his place in battery as soon as the reverse is completed and the carriages are on the line.

When the battery is marching in line, with the pieces in front, the formation in battery to the rear is executed according to the same principles and by the same commands. At the command IN BATTERY, which is given as soon as the caissons have passed their pieces, the latter halt, and the movement is completed as already described.

IN LINE, WITH CAISSONS IN FRONT, TO FORM IN BATTERY TO THE REAR.

When the battery is in line at a halt, with the caissons in front, to form in battery to the rear, the captain commands:

1. *Fire to the rear.* 2. IN BATTERY.

FIGURE 53. At the command IN BATTERY, which is repeated by the chiefs of sections, the cannoneers unlimber and prepare for firing.

The chiefs of pieces and sections take their places in battery.

The caissons move at a brisk trot and take their

places in battery, under the superintendence of their chief.

When the battery is marching in line, with the caissons in front, the formation in battery to the rear is executed according to the same principles and by the same commands.

IN BATTERY, TO FORM IN LINE TO THE FRONT.

Being in battery, to form in line to the front, with the caissons in rear, the captain commands:

LIMBER TO THE FRONT.

This command is repeated by the chiefs of sections, and the pieces are limbered as described in the School of the Piece; the caissons closing at the same time to the proper distance without further command.

When the captain wishes to place the caissons in front, he commands: LIMBER TO THE FRONT; and, while the pieces are limbering, *Caissons, pass your pieces — trot —* MARCH. The caissons pass, and halt in front of their pieces; or, if the captain wishes the battery to advance, he commands: FORWARD — *Guide right* (or *left*) as the caissons are completing the passage.

The commands are repeated by the chiefs of sections.

When the pieces can not be wheeled about by hand, the captain commands: LIMBER TO THE REAR; and, when this is executed, if he wishes to retain the pieces in front, he commands:

1. *Pieces, left about — caissons, forward.* 2. MARCH. 3. *Battery —* HALT.

FIGURE 54. The command LIMBER TO THE REAR is

repeated by the chiefs of sections. The first and second commands are also repeated by the chiefs of sections, and the pieces execute the about; the caissons closing at the same time to *two* yards. The third command is given as soon as the about is completed, and the word HALT being repeated by the chiefs of sections the pieces halt, and place themselves squarely on the line.

The captain rectifies the alignment, if necessary, and commands: FRONT.

When the battery is to advance immediately, the captain commands: FORWARD— *Guide right* (or *left*) instead of *Battery*—HALT; and the caissons close on the march.

FIGURE 55. When the captain wishes to place the caissons in front, he may cause the pieces to be limbered to the rear as before, and commands:

1. *Caissons, pass your pieces — trot — pieces, left about.* 2. MARCH. 3. *Battery*—HALT, or FORWARD—*Guide right* (or *left*).

These commands are repeated.

The pieces execute the about at once, the caissons move straight to the front, and so pass the pieces during the execution of the about.

IN BATTERY, TO FORM IN LINE TO THE REAR.

When in battery, to form in line to the rear, the captain causes the pieces to be limbered to the rear; and then, if he wishes to place the caissons in front, commands:

1. *Caissons, left about — pieces, forward.* 2. MARCH. 3. *Battery*—HALT, or FORWARD—*Guide right* (or *left*).

FIGURE 56. The first two commands are repeated by the chiefs of sections; the caissons execute the about, and the pieces close to their proper distances. The third command, which is given at the moment the about is finished, is repeated and executed as prescribed.

The captain rectifies the alignment if necessary, and commands: FRONT.

If the formation in line to the rear is to be executed by placing the pieces in front, the captain, after causing the pieces to be limbered to the rear, commands:

1. *Pieces, pass your caissons—caissons, left about.* 2. MARCH. 3. *Battery*—HALT, or FORWARD—*Guide right* (or *left*).

FIGURE 57. The first two commands are repeated by the chiefs of sections; at the command MARCH, the pieces pass their caissons by moving direct to the front, the caissons executing the about at the same command, and so regulating the gait as to take their proper distances.

The captain rectifies the alignment if necessary, and commands: FRONT.

In forming line to the rear, the caissons may be placed at once either in front or in rear of their pieces. To effect this the captain commands: LIMBER TO THE REAR, and immediately adds, to place them in front:

1. *Caissons, in front of your pieces* (or *Caissons, in front of your pieces—trot*). 2. MARCH.

While the pieces are limbering, the caissons oblique to the right, move forward near the middle of the interval between the leaders of the pieces, place themselves in front of them by two successive wheels to the left, and halt.

If he wishes to place them in rear, the commands are :

1. *Caissons, in rear of your pieces* (or *Caissons, in rear of your pieces—trot*). 2. MARCH.

The caissons incline to the right, pass their pieces, move sufficiently to the rear, and then by a *left reverse* take their positions in rear of their pieces.

The commands in both cases are repeated by the chiefs of sections.

IN COLUMN, WITH PIECES IN FRONT, TO FORM IN BATTERY TO THE FRONT.

When the battery is in column at a halt, with the pieces in front, to form in battery to the front, by gaining ground to the left, the captain commands:

1. *Forward into battery—left oblique.* 2. MARCH. 3. *Guide right.*

FIGURE 58. At the first command the chief of the leading section commands: *Section — forward ;* and those of the other sections: *Section—left oblique.* The chief of the line of caissons moves quickly to the right of the leading section, to cause the caissons to halt at the proper time and to superintend their alignment. At the command MARCH, repeated by the chiefs of sections, the movement is executed as prescribed for forming line to the front. But, as each section arrives on the line, instead of halting, its chief forms it in battery to the front by the commands: IN BATTERY—MARCH.

The formation in battery to the front, by gaining

ground to the right, is executed according to the same principles, and by inverse means. The commands are:

Forward into battery—right oblique — MARCH *— Guide left.*

When the battery is marching in column, it is formed in battery to the front by applying the same principles.

IN COLUMN, WITH CAISSONS IN FRONT, TO FORM IN BATTERY TO THE FRONT.

When the battery is in column at a halt, with the caissons in front, to form in battery to the front, by gaining ground to the left, the captain commands:

1. *Forward into battery—left oblique.* 2. MARCH. 3. *Guide right.*

FIGURE 59. At the first command the chief of the leading section commands: *Section — forward;* and those of the other sections: *Section—left oblique.* The chief of the line of caissons moves quickly to the right of the leading section, to halt the caissons at the proper time and to superintend their alignment. At the command MARCH, repeated by the chiefs of sections, the movement is executed as prescribed for forming line to the front. But, as each section arrives on the line, instead of halting, its chief forms it in battery to the front by the commands: *Pieces, pass your caissons—*MARCH*—*IN BATTERY*—*MARCH.

The formation in battery to the front, by gaining ground to the right, is executed according to the same principles, and by inverse means.

When the battery is marching in column, it is

formed in battery to the front by applying the same principles.

In Column, with Pieces in Front, to Form in Battery to the Rear.

When the battery is in column at a halt, with the pieces in front, to form in battery to the rear, by gaining ground to the left, the captain commands:

1. *Into battery, faced to the rear—left oblique.* 2. March. 3. *Guide right.*

Figure 60. At the first command the chief of the leading section commands: *Section — forward;* and those of the other sections: *Section—left oblique.* The chief of the line of caissons goes to the right of the leading section, to direct the reverse of the caissons and to superintend their alignment. At the command March, repeated by the chiefs of sections, the movement is executed as prescribed for forming line to the front. But, as each section arrives on the line, instead of halting, its chief forms it in battery to the rear by the commands: *Fire to the rear—Caissons, pass your pieces—trot—*March*—*In battery.

The formation in battery to the rear, by gaining ground to the right, is executed according to the same principles, and by inverse means.

When the battery is marching in column, it is formed into battery to the rear by applying the same principles.

In Column, with Caissons in Front, to Form in Battery to the Rear.

The battery being in column at a halt, with the

caissons in front, to form in battery to the rear, by gaining ground to the left, the captain commands:

1. *Into battery, faced to the rear—left oblique.* 2. MARCH. 3. *Guide right.*

FIGURE 61. At the first command the chief of the leading section commands: *Section —forward;* and those of the other sections: *Section—left oblique.* The chief of the line of caissons goes to the right of the leading section, to direct the about of the caissons and to superintend their alignment. At the command MARCH, repeated by the chiefs of sections, the movement is executed as prescribed for forming line to the front. But, as each section arrives on the line, instead of halting, its chief forms it into battery to the rear by the commands: *Fire to the rear—*IN BATTERY.

The formation in battery to the rear, by gaining ground to the right, is executed according to the same principles, and by inverse means.

When the battery is marching in column, it is formed into battery to the rear by applying the same principles.

IN COLUMN, WITH PIECES IN FRONT, TO FORM IN BATTERY TO THE RIGHT OR LEFT.

When the battery is in column, in march or at a halt, with the pieces in front, if the captain wishes to form it in battery to the left, by gaining ground to the right, he commands:

1. *Fire to the left—by section, right wheel.* 2. MARCH. 3. *Caissons, pass your pieces—trot.* 4. MARCH. 5. IN BATTERY.

FIGURE 62. At the first command the chiefs of the

sections command: *Section—right wheel;* and at the second, which they repeat, all the sections wheel to the right. The caissons follow their pieces at the proper distance.

At the commands *Caissons, pass your pieces—trot—* MARCH, which are given before the completion of the wheel, and repeated by the chiefs of sections, all the caissons pass their pieces at a trot.

At the command IN BATTERY, which is given and repeated in like manner as soon as the caissons have passed and the pieces are square on the new line, all the sections form at once into battery to the rear.

When the captain wishes to form in battery to the left, by gaining ground to the left, he commands:

1. *Fire to the left—by section, left wheel.* 2. MARCH.
3. IN BATTERY. 4. MARCH.

FIGURE 63. At the first command the chiefs of sections command: *Section — left wheel;* and at the second, which they repeat, all the sections wheel at once to the left.

At the command IN BATTERY, which is given and repeated as soon as the caissons have completed the wheel, all the sections form at once into battery to the front.

The two formations in battery to the right, by gaining ground to the left or right, are executed according to the same principles, and by inverse means. The commands are: *Fire to the right—by section, left wheel* — MARCH; *caissons, pass your pieces— trot — march* — IN BATTERY; or, *Fire to the right — by section, right wheel* — MARCH — IN BATTERY — MARCH. (Figure 64.)

IN COLUMN, WITH CAISSONS IN FRONT, TO FORM IN BATTERY TO THE RIGHT OR LEFT.

When the battery is in column, in march or at a halt, with the caissons in front, to form it in battery to the left, by gaining ground to the right, the captain commands:

1. *Fire to the left — by section, right wheel.* 2. MARCH. 3. IN BATTERY.

FIGURE 65. At the first command the chiefs of sections command: *Section — right wheel;* and at the second, which they repeat, the sections wheel at once to the right, and move to the front at the commands FORWARD—*Guide right* from their chiefs.

At the command IN BATTERY, which is given and repeated as soon as the pieces are square on the new line, all the sections form at once into battery to the rear.

To form in battery to the left, gaining ground to the left, the captain commands:

1. *Fire to the left — by section, left wheel.* 2. MARCH. 3. *Pieces, pass your caissons.* 4. MARCH. 5. IN BATTERY. 6. MARCH.

FIGURE 66. At the first command the chiefs of sections command: *Section — left wheel;* and at the second, which they repeat, the sections wheel at once to the left. The third and fourth commands are given and repeated just before the completion of the wheel; and the fifth is given when the pieces have passed their caissons and the latter are square upon the new line. The sections are then formed in battery to the front.

The formation in battery to the right, by gaining

ground to the right or left, are executed according to the same principles, and by inverse means. (Figure 67.)

In Column, with Pieces in Front, to Form in Battery on the Right or Left.

When the battery is marching in column, with the pieces in front, to form in battery on the right, the captain commands:

1. *On the right into battery.* 2. MARCH. 3. *Guide right.*

At the first command the chief of the leading section commands: *Section — right wheel;* and the chief of the line of caissons goes to that section. At the command MARCH, repeated by the chief of the leading section, that section wheels to the right, and its chief conducts it to the line by the commands FORWARD—*Guide right.* And then, without halting, it is formed into battery to the front, by the commands IN BATTERY—MARCH—from its chief.

The other sections continue to advance; and, as each arrives opposite its place in battery, after passing the one preceding it in the formation, it is formed into battery by its chief, by the commands *Section — right wheel*—MARCH—FORWARD—*Guide right*—IN BATTERY—MARCH; the command IN BATTERY being given as the caissons arrive in line with those already established.

The formation in battery on the left is executed according to the same principles, and by inverse means.

When the battery is in column at a halt, it is formed in battery on the right or left according to the same principles. In this case, the chiefs of the two rear sections command: *Section—forward* immediately after the first command of the captain, and then repeat the commands MARCH—*Guide right* (or *left*).

IN COLUMN, WITH CAISSONS IN FRONT, TO FORM IN BATTERY ON THE RIGHT OR LEFT.

When the battery is marching in column, with the caissons in front, to form in battery on the right, the captain commands:

1. *On the right into battery.* 2. MARCH. 3. *Guide right.*

At the first command the chief of the leading section commands: *Section—right wheel;* and the chief of the line of caissons goes to that section. At the command MARCH, repeated by the chief of the leading section, that section wheels to the right, and is conducted to the line by the commands FORWARD—*Guide right* from its chief; as soon as it reaches the line, the section is formed in battery to the front by the commands *Pieces, pass your caissons*—MARCH—IN BATTERY—MARCH from its chief.

The other sections continue to advance, and, as each arrives opposite its place in battery, after having passed the one preceding it in the formation, it is wheeled to the right, and formed into battery by its chief, in the same manner as the leading section.

The formation in battery on the left is executed according to the same principles, and by inverse means.

When the battery is in column at a halt, it is formed in battery on the right or left according to the same principles.

11

To Deploy the Double Column into Battery to the Front or Rear.

The battery being in double column at a halt, to deploy it into battery to the front, the captain commands:

1. *Forward into battery.* 2. MARCH.

At the first command the chief of the centre section commands: *Section—forward;* that of the right: *Section—into line—right oblique;* that of the left: *Section into line—left oblique;* and the chief of the line of caissons goes to the leading section. At the command MARCH, repeated by the chiefs of sections, the centre section advances *five* yards, and, without halting, is formed into battery to the front.

The pieces of the flank sections are brought upon the line by obliquing, and placed successively in battery without command; regulating by the centre section.

When the battery is marching in double column, it is deployed into battery to the front in the same manner, except that the chief of the centre section does not command *Section—forward—*MARCH.

When the battery is in double column, marching or at a halt, it is deployed into battery to the rear according to the same principles. The commands are:

1. *Into battery, faced to the rear.* 2. MARCH.

When the battery consists of four or eight pieces, the double column is deployed into battery to the front or rear by the same commands from the captain as when it consisted of six. The sections are formed into battery as prescribed for the flank sections in this number. The leading chief of section, besides superintending the formation of his own, gives the commands required for the centre section, and the leading pieces conform to the movements of that section.

To Deploy the Double Column into Battery to the Right or Left.

When the battery is in double column, marching or at a halt, to form it in battery to the right, the captain commands:

1. *To and on the right into battery.* 2. March.

The centre section is formed in battery on the right as prescribed for the leading section.

The other pieces are brought into line, and, without halting, are formed successively in battery to the front without commands; regulating by the centre section.

The deployment into battery to the left is executed according to the same principles, and by inverse means.

When the battery consists of four or eight pieces, the column is deployed into battery to the right or left by the same commands from the captain as when it consists of six. In this case, the leading pieces are wheeled to the right or left as a section, and conducted to the line by the leading chief of section. And then, without halting, they are formed into battery to the front by the same chief. The other pieces move forward, wheel in succession as they arrive opposite their places, and form in battery on the alignment of those already established.

To Pass from the Order in Battery to the Order in Column.

Being in battery, to form column, the captain first causes the line to be formed, and then forms column by one of the manœuvres for passing from the order in line to the order in column.

To March by a Flank.

Being in battery, to gain ground to the left, for the purpose of forming again in battery without an intermediate formation, the captain causes the pieces to be limbered to the rear, and commands:

1. *Pieces, right—caissons, left—wheel.* 2. March. 3. Forward. 4. *Guide right.*

Figure 68. These commands are repeated by the chiefs of sections.

The movement to gain ground to the left may be executed by limbering at once to the left; the caissons wheeling to the left while the pieces are limbering; and the captain afterward commanding: *Forward*—March—*Guide right.*

The movement to gain ground to the right is executed by either of the methods above described, applying the same principles, and by inverse means.

As soon as the battery has reached the position on the left which it is intended to occupy, the captain commands:

1. *Battery, by the left flank.* 2. March. 3. *Fire to the rear.* 4. In battery.

The commands *By the left flank*—March are repeated by the chiefs of sections, and executed as usual. The commands *Fire to the rear*—In battery are given and repeated as soon as the pieces have completed the wheel, and executed as prescribed.

When the battery is to move to a flank, and be formed into battery again on the same line, it may be executed by limbering to the front, marching to a flank, and then commanding: *Column—by the right* (or *left) flank*—MARCH—*Fire to the rear*—IN BATTERY; the caissons taking their proper places in battery by a left about.

The same thing may be executed by limbering to the right or left, gaining ground to the flank, halting, and commanding: ACTION LEFT, or ACTION RIGHT.

ARTICLE VI.

FIRINGS.

When everything is prepared for firing, the captain commands:

COMMENCE FIRING.

This command, given by itself or after LOAD, is repeated by the chiefs of sections, and the firing is immediately commenced.

To fire by battery, the captain commands:

1. *Fire by battery.* 2. *Battery*—FIRE.

The first command is repeated by the chiefs of sections; the second is not repeated.

To fire by half-battery, the commands of the captain are:

1. *Fire by half-battery.* 2. *Right* (or *left*) *half-battery*—
FIRE.

To fire by section :

1. *Fire by section.* 2. *Right (centre or left) section—* FIRE.

To fire by piece :

1. *Fire by piece.* 2. *Right section—right (or left) piece—* FIRE.

The chiefs of half-batteries or sections repeat the first command, and immediately designate their respective commands as *Right* or *left* half-battery— *Right* or *left* section. They do not repeat the second commands.

The firing is discontinued by the command or signal:

CEASE FIRING.

This command is repeated by the chiefs of sections and of pieces, and the loaded pieces discharged or the load drawn, except in the case when the battery is retiring with the prolonge.

To move and fire with the prolonge fixed, the captain gives the necessary directions. It is but seldom that this mode of moving and firing is necessary, and it will only be resorted to when circumstances require it.

TO FIRE ADVANCING.

When the battery is firing, to advance by half-batteries, the captain commands :

1. *Fire advancing by half-battery.* 2. *Right half-battery—* ADVANCE.

At the second command the chief of the right half-battery discontinues firing, causes his pieces to be limbered to the front, and commands: *Forward—* MARCH—*Guide left.* Or he may cause them to be limbered to the rear, and, after executing the about, command: FORWARD—*Guide left.* The half-battery advances, and the caissons preserve their distance in battery.

As soon as the right half-battery reaches the new position, previously indicated by the captain, its chief places it in battery by the commands HALT—ACTION FRONT; or, IN BATTERY—MARCH; the two last commands being given in quick succession. The caissons halt at these commands, and, as soon as the pieces are unlimbered, the firing is renewed by command from the chief of half-battery.

The fire of the left half-battery is continued during the movement of the right, care being taken to direct the pieces so that their fire shall not injure the half-battery in advance.

As soon as the right half-battery commences firing the left moves forward with the guide to the right; and, after passing the right half-battery as far as the latter has advanced, is formed into battery and the firing commenced. The movements of the left half-battery are effected by commands and means corresponding to those of the right.

The right half-battery again advances as soon as the left commences firing, and the two continue to advance alternately until the captain causes the firing to cease. The battery is then aligned, or formed into line to the front or rear, by the proper commands from the captain.

While advancing by half-battery, the captain places himself habitually with the most advanced portion of the battery; and in six-gun batteries is accompanied by the chief of the centre section. The chief of the line of caissons remains habitually with the rear half-battery.

To fire advancing by half-battery, commencing with the left, is executed according to the same principles, and by inverse means.

The movement may also be executed by section; the sections advancing in succession according to their positions in the battery.

To Fire in Retreat.

When the battery is firing, to retire by half-batteries, the captain commands:

1. *Fire retiring by half-battery.* 2. *Right half-battery.* 3. Retire.

At the second command the chief of the right half-battery discontinues firing, limbers to the rear, and commands: *Caissons, left about*—March. As soon as the about is completed, he commands: Forward—*Guide right*, and conducts the half-battery to the ground previously indicated by the captain; the pieces preserving their distance in battery by marching *nineteen* yards in rear of the caissons. As soon as the ground has been reached, the chief of half-battery commands: Halt—*Fire to the rear*—In battery, and commences firing; taking care not to injure the other half-battery. The limbers and caissons remain facing toward the rear as long as the firing in retreat continues.

As soon as the right half-battery commences firing the left retires with the guide to the left; and, after passing the right half-battery as far as the latter has retired, it is formed into battery, and the firing again commenced. The movements are executed in a manner corresponding to those of the other half-battery.

The half-batteries continue to retire alternately

until the captain causes the firing to cease. The battery is afterward aligned, or formed into line to the front or rear, by appropriate commands from the captain.

While retiring by half-battery the captain remains habitually with the portion of the battery nearest the enemy, and is accompanied by the chief of the centre section. The chief of the line of caissons accompanies the other half-battery.

To fire retiring by half-battery, commencing with the left, is executed according to the same principles, and by inverse means.

The movement may also be executed by sections; the sections retiring in succession, according to their positions in the battery.

MOVEMENTS FOR FIRING IN ECHELON.

When the battery is in line at a halt, with pieces in front, to advance in echelon of pieces, the captain commands:

1. *By piece from the right—front into echelon.* 2. MARCH.

FIGURE 69. At the last command the right piece moves forward, followed by its caisson. The next piece moves forward in like manner as soon as its leaders are abreast the wheel-horses of the rear carriage on the right; and the other pieces commence the movement in succession according to the same rule.

The officers preserve the same relative positions as in line.

When the battery is marching in line, at a walk or trot, the echelon is formed according to the same principles, and by the same commands; the gaits being regulated as in breaking sections. The battery advances in echelon of pieces from the left according to the same principles, and by inverse means.

When the caissons are in front, the battery advances in echelon of pieces from the right or left according to the same principles, and by the same commands.

When the battery is in echelon, marching or at a halt, it may be formed into battery to the front, rear, right, or left.

When firing in echelon to the front or rear, the direction of the fire may be changed to the right or left. For this purpose the captain orders the firing to cease, and commands: ACTION RIGHT (OR LEFT). At this command the trails of the pieces are turned to the left (or right), and the limbers and caissons take their places in rear of the pieces. But if retiring with the prolonge fixed, the caissons stand fast, and the limbers back to allow the trails to be turned in the proper direction. The prolonge must be sufficiently slack to allow the recoil of the guns. This last method is only applicable to firing to the right when retiring by the right, and to the left when retiring by the left.

BEING IN ECHELON, TO FORM LINE.

The battery being in echelon at a halt, to form it into line, the captain commands:

1. *On the right* (or *left*) *piece — forward into line.*
2. MARCH.

The commands are repeated by the chiefs of sections. Each piece moves forward and establishes itself on the line, dressing on the piece indicated.

SCHOOL OF THE BATTERY. 131

If the battery is in march, to form the line without halting, the commands are:

1. *Form line advancing, on right* (or *left*) *piece — trot.*
2. MARCH.

The pieces to the rear move forward at the increased gait, and take their positions in line.

If the battery is in echelon and firing, to form it in the order in battery, continuing the fire, the captain causes the pieces behind the line on which the formation is to be made to cease their fire, and commands:

1. *On the right* (or *left*) *piece — forward into battery.*
2. MARCH.

At the first command the chief of the right section places his left piece on the line, the right continuing its fire. The chiefs of the other sections cause them to be limbered to the front, and at the command MARCH, which they repeat, move them forward, and establish them in battery on a line with the right section.

TO FIRE TO THE REAR.

When the battery is firing, to fire in the opposite direction, the captain causes the firing to cease, and commands:

1. *Fire to the rear.* 2. *Limbers and caissons, pass your pieces—trot.* 3. MARCH.

FIGURE 70. These commands are repeated by the chiefs of sections. At the command MARCH, the pieces are wheeled about by turning the trails to the left; and the limbers and caissons oblique to the right, pass them, and take their places in battery by a left reverse.

When the pieces can not be wheeled about by hand, the captain commands:

1. *Fire to the rear.* 2. LIMBER TO THE REAR. 3. *Caissons, pass your pieces — trot —* MARCH. 4. *Pieces, left about —* MARCH. 5. IN BATTERY.

ARTICLE VII.

CHANGES OF FRONT IN BATTERY.

CHANGE OF FRONT TO FIRE TO THE RIGHT, LEFT WING FORWARD, AND THE REVERSE.

When the battery is firing, if the captain wishes to make a perpendicular change of front, to fire to the right, throwing forward the left wing, he discontinues firing, and commands:

1. *Fire to the right.* 2. *Change front forward on the right piece.* 3. MARCH.

FIGURE 71. At the second command the chief of the right section places the right piece in the new direction, by causing the trail to be moved to the left. He also causes the left piece of his section to be moved forward by hand, and established on the new line. When the ground is unmasked, the limbers and caissons of these pieces oblique to the left, move forward, and take their places in battery by wheeling to the right; the caissons aligning themselves by the chief of the line of caissons established on the right.

The other chiefs of sections cause their pieces to be limbered by the command LIMBER TO THE FRONT; the caissons closing upon the pieces while they are limbering. As soon as they are limbered, the chiefs of sections command: *Forward.*

At the second command the chief of the line of caissons places himself on the left of the right piece of the centre section, facing to the front, to mark the right of the new line of caissons.

At the command MARCH, repeated by the chiefs of the centre and left sections, these sections move to the front; and, when each has arrived opposite its place on the new line, its chief commands: *Section — right wheel —* MARCH *—* FORWARD; and afterward, *In battery —* MARCH, so as to form upon the alignment of the right section. When the caisson of the right piece of the centre section reaches the point where its piece wheeled, it wheels to the left, takes its distance in rear, wheels about, and dresses to the right upon the line of caissons.

The other caisson of the same section obliques to the left when its piece commences the wheel; and, after gaining its distance, establishes itself on the line by wheeling and dressing to the right.

When the pieces are too heavy to be moved or wheeled about by hand, the chiefs of sections cause them to be limbered, with the exception of the right piece, by the command LIMBER TO THE REAR. The chief of the right section then commands: *Piece, left about — caisson, forward;* and the chiefs of the other sections: *Pieces, left about — caissons, forward.* At the command MARCH, repeated by the chiefs of sections, the pieces are wheeled about and directed to the front by the command FORWARD from the chiefs of sections. The left piece of the right section is established on the line by the commands *Right wheel —* MARCH *—* FORWARD *— In battery —* MARCH from the chief of the section. The caisson wheels to the left when it reaches the point where its piece wheeled to the right; and, after taking its distance, wheels about and dresses to the right upon the chief of the line of caissons. The other sections are established upon the line as already described.

The pivot piece commences firing again as soon as it is in position, and the others as they arrive on the line.

The change of front to fire to the left, right wing forward, is executed according to the same principles, and by inverse means.

Change of Front to Fire to the Left, Left Wing Forward, and the Reverse.

When the battery is firing, if the captain wishes to make a perpendicular change of front to fire to the left, throwing forward the left wing, he discontinues firing, and commands:

1. *Fire to the left.* 2. *Change front forward on the right piece.* 4. March.

At the second command the chief of the right section causes the right piece to be placed in the new direction at once, by moving the trail to the right; and the limber and caisson of that piece will oblique to the right, and take their places in its rear by wheeling to the left; the caisson dressing upon the chief of the line of caissons. He also causes his left piece to be moved to its place and established on the line by hand; the limber of this piece, passing it on the right, takes its place by wheeling to the left, its caisson obliques to the right, passes on the right, and in rear of the right caisson, and takes its place also by wheeling to the left.

The chiefs of the other sections cause them to be limbered to the front; and while limbering they command: *Caissons, pass your pieces—trot—*MARCH. When this is executed, the chief of the centre section commands: *Section — right wheel,* and that of the left: *Forward.*

At the command MARCH, repeated by the chiefs of the centre and left sections, these sections move as ordered, with the caissons leading. The centre section is conducted to the line by its chief, and formed by the commands FORWARD and IN BATTERY. The left section advances *five* yards, and is conducted to the line by two successive right half-wheels. It is there formed in like manner upon the alignment of the right section.

At the second command from the captain, the chief of the line of caissons places himself in prolongation of the line, *thirty-two* yards on the right of the right piece, and faces to the front to mark the left of the new line of caissons.

When the pieces are too heavy to be wheeled about or moved by hand, the chiefs of sections cause them to be limbered to the rear, with the exception of the right piece. While the pieces are limbering, the chiefs of the centre and left sections cause the caissons to pass as before; and all the chiefs of sections give the cautionary command for their pieces to wheel about. At the command MARCH, repeated by the chiefs of sections, the pieces are wheeled about, and the sections conducted to the new line by the appropriate commands. The caisson of the left piece of the right section takes its place in the same manner as when its piece is moved by hand.

The pivot piece recommences firing as soon as it is

unmasked; and the others when they arrive on the line.

The change of front to fire to the right, right wing forward, is executed according to the same principles, and by inverse means.

CHANGE OF FRONT TO FIRE TO THE LEFT, LEFT WING TO THE REAR, AND THE REVERSE.

When the battery is firing, if the captain wishes to make a perpendicular change of front to fire to the left, throwing the left wing to the rear, he causes the firing to cease, and commands:

1. *Fire to the left.* 2. *Change front to the rear on the right piece.* 3. MARCH.

At the second command the chief of the right section places the right piece in the new direction, by causing the trail to be moved to the right. He also causes the left piece of his section to be moved to the rear by hand and established on the new line. The limbers and caissons of these pieces move at once to the right, obliquing sufficiently to place themselves in rear of their respective pieces, and take their places by wheeling or reversing to the left.

The other chiefs of sections command: *Limber to the rear;* and immediately afterward: *Caissons, in front of your pieces — trot —* MARCH. The caissons place themselves in front of their pieces while they are limbering, and halt. The chief of the centre section then commands: *Section — left wheel;* that of the left section: *Section—forward.*

The chief of the line of caissons places himself in the prolongation of the line *thirty-two* yards on the right piece, and faces to the rear to mark the right of the new line of caissons.

At the command MARCH, given by the captain, and repeated by the chiefs of the centre and left sections, those sections are put in motion and placed in battery on the line, the chief of the left section wheeling it to the left when it is opposite its position.

When the pieces are too heavy to be moved by hand, the chief of the right section causes his left piece to be limbered to the rear with the rest, and then commands: *Left wheel.* At the command MARCH, repeated by this chief, the piece wheels to the left, and is conducted by him to its place by the commands FORWARD—IN BATTERY. The caisson takes its place as before described.

The pivot piece recommences firing as soon as it is unmasked; and the others when they arrive on the line.

The change of front to fire to the right, right wing to the rear, is executed according to the same principles, and by inverse means.

CHANGE OF FRONT TO FIRE TO THE RIGHT, LEFT WING TO THE REAR, AND THE REVERSE.

FIGURE 72. When the battery is firing, if the captain wishes to make a perpendicular change of front to fire to the right, throwing the left wing to the rear, he discontinues firing, and commands:

1. *Fire to the right.* 2. *Change front to the rear on the right piece.* 3. MARCH.

At the second command the chief of the right section commands: *Limbers and caissons, in rear of your pieces — trot —* MARCH. The limbers and caissons oblique to the right, and pass their pieces, with the limbers leading. As soon as the limbers have passed, they wheel twice to the left and cover their pieces. The caissons pass their limbers and cover them in like manner. The chief of the section causes the trail of his right piece to be moved to the left, and his left piece to be placed upon the new alignment by hand.

The chiefs of the other sections command: LIMBER TO THE REAR, and *Caissons, in rear to your pieces—trot*—MARCH. When this is executed, they command: *Forward*.

At the second command the chief of the line of caissons places himself on the left of the right piece of the centre section, facing to the rear, to mark the left of the new line of caissons.

At the command MARCH, from the captain, repeated by the chiefs of the centre and left sections, those sections, as well as the limbers and caissons of the first, are established upon the new line.

When the piece can not be moved by hand, the chief of the right section causes his left piece to be limbered like the rest; and then causes the remaining limber and the caissons to pass as before described. When the piece is limbered, he commands: *Left wheel*. At the command MARCH, from the captain, repeated by the chiefs of sections, the piece is wheeled and conducted to its place on the line.

The pivot piece recommences firing as soon as it is placed in the new direction; and the others as they arrive on the line.

The change of front to fire to the left, right wing to the rear, is executed according to the same principles, and by inverse means.

To Pass a Defile in Front.

When the battery is firing, to pass a defile in front of the right section, the captain commands:

1. *To the front—by the right section—pass the defile.*
2. March.

At the first command the chief of the right section discontinues firing, limbers his piece to the front, and commands: *Forward.* At the command March, repeated by this chief, who also commands *Guide left*, the section moves forward, passes the defile, and is again established in battery, and the firing commenced by his command.

When the pieces are too heavy to be wheeled about by hand, the chief of the section causes them to be limbered to the rear, wheeled about, and the caissons closed, before giving the command *Forward*.

As soon as the right section commences firing, the centre is put in motion in like manner. Its chief conducts it through the defile by successive wheels, and forms it into battery in line with the first.

As soon as the centre section commences firing, the left passes in like manner.

While one section is passing the defile, the others continue firing; care being taken not to injure the section in advance.

When the defile is in front of the left section, it is passed according to the same principles, commencing with that section.

When the defile is in front of the centre section, it is passed according to the same principles, commencing with that section, and by the commands: *To the front —by the centre section —pass the defile—* March.

Unless there is some reason to the contrary, the right section will pass before the left.

When the flank or oblique march is better suited to the nature of the ground, the chiefs of sections will give the required commands.

When the defile will admit but one piece at a time, the sections are broken by their chiefs in such a manner as to cause the nearest piece to enter first. The sections are reformed by their chiefs immediately after passing the defile.

To Pass a Defile in Rear.

When the battery is firing, to pass a defile in rear of the centre section, the captain commands:

1. *To the rear—by the right section—pass the defile.*
2. March.

At the first command the chief of the right section discontinues firing, the limbers to the rear, and commands: *Caissons, left about — pieces, forward.* At the command March, repeated by the chief of the right section, the caissons of that section execute the about, and the pieces close to their proper distance at a trot. As soon as the about is completed, the chief commands: Forward — *Guide left,* conducts the section through the defile by successive wheels, and forms it into battery in rear of its first position.

The left section is put in motion as soon as the right commences firing. It is conducted through the defile by its chief, and formed into battery in rear of its first position, by the principles already described.

The centre section moves as soon as the left commences firing. It is formed into battery in rear of its first position, and in line with the other two sections.

The passage of the defile may be executed, commencing with the left section, according to the same principles, and by inverse means.

When the defile is in rear of one of the flanks, the movement should commence with the other. It should always end by passing the section or piece covering the defile.

When the defile will admit but one piece at a time, the sections are broken by their chiefs in such a manner as to cause the piece farthest from the defile to enter first; and the sections are again formed as soon as possible after leaving the defile.

Parade for Review and Inspection.

The battery being in line, with the pieces in front; the first sergeant *two* yards from the right; the bugler and guidon in one rank, *six* yards on his right; the quartermaster-sergeant *two* yards from the left; the artificers in one rank, *six* yards on his left; all dressed on the lead-drivers of pieces; the captain commands:

1. Attention. 2. *Prepare for review.* 3. Action front. 4. *Right* Dress. 5. Front.

At the third command the battery is formed as directed; the chiefs of sections take their places in the centres of the sections, *three* yards in front of the line of muzzles; and the chiefs of pieces, without dismounting, take their places at their posts, *in battery*. The non-commissioned staff, buglers, guidon, and artificers reverse with their limbers, and take their places, in the order already directed, on a line with the lead-drivers; the cannoneers are at their posts.

At the fourth command the battery is aligned—the chiefs of the sections, the pieces, and the limbers by the captain; and the caissons by the chief of the line of caissons.

At the fifth command, given by the captain when the alignment is completed, the chief of the line of caissons takes this position *in battery*. The captain then commands:

Draw—SABRES.

This is executed by the staff sergeants, chiefs of pieces, and artificers only; and the captain takes post *twelve* yards in front of the centre of the battery (*eight* yards, if there are two or more batteries in line), faces to the front, and awaits the approach of the reviewing officer.

When the reviewing officer is midway between the camp-color and the captain, the latter reverses to the right, and commands:

Present—SABRES.

He immediately resumes his front and salutes, as do all whose sabres are drawn; and the music plays according to the rank of the reviewing officer.

The reviewing officer having halted, and acknowledged the salute, the captain brings his sword to a carry, reverses as before, and commands:

Carry—SABRES.

He immediately resumes his front; the reviewing officer turns off to the right of the battery, passes along its front, and returns to the right by passing between the lines of carriages, or in rear of the caisson.

While the reviewing officer is passing around the battery, the music plays. It ceases when he turns off to take his post at the camp-color.

When the music ceases, the captain faces the battery, and commands:

Limber to the Front,

and all assume their places in line.

The reviewing officer having taken a position near the camp-color, the captain causes the cannoneers to mount, and breaks the battery into column of sections to the right by the usual commands.

He then commands:

Pass in Review,

and puts the column in march, at a walk, with the guide to the right.

The captain then places himself at the head of the column, *four* yards in advance of the chief of the leading section; the trumpeters or buglers march *four* yards in advance of the captain; the chief of the line of caissons outside the column, opposite the centre, and *four* yards from the left flank; the first sergeant and quartermaster-sergeant outside the column, *four* yards from the left flank, the former abreast the lead-drivers of the leading section, the latter abreast the lead-drivers of the rear section; the artificers in one rank, *four* yards in rear of the column; the guidon at the side of the chief of the directing piece.

When the head of the column has arrived within *forty* yards of the reviewing officer the music begins to play, and as soon as the latter has passed it wheels out of the column to a position in front of the reviewing officer, where it faces him, and continues to play until the column has passed. It then ceases, follows in rear of the battery, and resumes its place at the head of the column after the next change of direction.

All the officers salute in succession as they arrive within *six* yards of the reviewing officer, casting their eyes toward him at the same time, and bringing their sabres to a carry after having passed him *six* yards. As soon as the captain has saluted, he places himself on the left of the reviewing officer, passing by his rear, remains until the battery has passed, and then rejoins it, again passing by the rear.

The column is so conducted as to march parallel to the line on which the battery is to form, and far enough in its rear to enable the column to wheel into line. It is then wheeled into line, formed in battery, and the review terminated by a salute as at the beginning.

When instructions have been previously given to pass a second time, either at a trot or gallop, it will be done before wheeling into line, the officers passing the second time without saluting.

At the command CLOSE ORDER, instead of limbering to the front, the captain commands:

1. LIMBER TO THE FRONT. 2. *Pieces, left about—Caissons, forward.* 3. MARCH. 4. *Battery*—HALT.

These commands are executed, and the pieces halt with their lead-drivers on a line with the other troops.

After passing in review, and reaching the ground on which it is to form, the battery may be wheeled by section to the right, and, after gaining the necessary distance to the rear, countermarched, and established on the line.

When a battery is to march past in line or in column of half-batteries, it will be done according to the principles already described. *In line,* the officers, etc., will be at their usual posts. *In column of half-batteries,* the captain will be *two* yards in advance of the chief of the leading half-battery; each chief of half-battery *two* yards in front of the centre of his command; the chief of the centre section on the left of the leading half-battery, *four* yards from its centre, and the chief of the line of caissons in the same position with respect to the rear half-battery.

In eight-gun batteries, when the column is formed by half-battery, the chiefs of sections who do not command half-batteries retain their places in their sections.

The buglers are *four* yards in front of the captain. The first sergeant and quartermaster-sergeant are outside the column of half-batteries, *four* yards from the left flank, the former abreast the lead-driver of the leading, the latter abreast the lead-driver of the rear half-battery, the artificers in one rank, *four* yards in rear of the column, the guidon at the side of the chief of the directing piece.

Officers' Salute with the Sabre.

When the officers are to salute, whether on horseback or on foot, at a halt or in march, they execute it in four motions:

1st. At *six* yards from the person to be saluted, raise the sabre perpendicularly, the point upward, edge to the left, the hand opposite to and *one* foot from the right shoulder, the wrist six inches from the body.

2d. Lower the blade, extending the arm to its full length, the hand *in quarte,* until the point of the sabre is near the foot.

3d. Raise the sabre quickly, the point upward as in

the first motion, after the person saluted is passed *four* yards.

4th. Bring the sabre to carry.

Inspection.

The batteries of field artillery will always, for inspection, be formed either in line or in battery.

The knapsacks of the cannoneers are strapped on the foot-boards of the ammunition-chests. If the inspector wishes to examine the clothing of the men on the field, the knapsacks and valises will be unstrapped, laid at the feet of the men, and opened, the drivers being dismounted for the purpose.

Part Third.

THE COMPANY DISMOUNTED.

Formation of the Company.

Figure 73. In the artillery, as no two men of a piece, cannoneers or drivers, perform the same duties, each should be specially assigned to that position for which he is best fitted.

The men, whether cannoneers or drivers, are permanently attached to the pieces, and will not be transferred except by order of the captain, or temporarily to equalize detachments on drill or parade.

The cannoneers assigned to the service of a gun constitute a *gun detachment*, and are commanded by the gunner. When the company is paraded, dismounted, these detachments fall in each on the right of the men of its piece — the cannoneers taking their places according to their numbers in the detachment.

When the cannoneers and drivers attached to a piece are assembled in rank and file formation, they constitute a *platoon*, which is commanded by the sergeant, who is chief of the piece. The drivers form on the left, and the platoon is divided into detachments of the same size as the gun detachment, the men being numbered in the same manner.

Two platoons constitute a *section*, which is commanded by a lieutenant.

The *company* is composed of two, three, or four

sections. The instruction laid down is applicable in either case, but is given for three sections. When there are four sections, the company is further divided into *divisions*, each composed of two sections, and commanded by its ranking chief of section. The company will not be manœuvred by *divisons* unless circumstances require it, the section or platoon being the most convenient subdivision for manœuvring.

The company is commanded by a captain. A subaltern, in addition to the chiefs of sections, is attached to it. He performs the staff duties of the battery, and commands the line of caissons in the battery formations. In addition to the platoons, there should be attached to the company one *sergeant-major* or *first sergeant;* one *quartermaster-sergeant;* two *buglers* or *trumpeters;* one *guidon;* and such number of *artificers* as the service of the battery may require. In the absence of the lieutenant, chief of the line of caissons, he is replaced by the first sergeant.

The platoons form when in line in the order of their pieces in park, and touching each other.

The two forming a section are designated as the right and left platoons, according to their actual positions with reference to each other in the sections.

When necessary, surplus men may be transferred from one platoon to another, so that there shall be but one incomplete detachment in the company, which should not be on the flank. When an incomplete detachment consists of an odd number of men, the vacancy is left in the rear rank, in the next file but one from the left, that number being omitted in calling off.

To prevent the formation of incomplete detachments, artificers may be assigned as No. 8; or the

THE COMPANY DISMOUNTED. 149

permanent chiefs of caissons may be assigned as gunners to detachments other than the gun detachment, and posted *one* yard behind the right files.

When the company is formed for parade purposes, and it is not desired to manœuvre by detachments, the platoons may be equalized, and regarded as the units. They are then formed as single detachments, the chiefs of the caissons being posted as the front rank men of the left files of the platoons. The men call off from No. 1 to No. 8, as if divided into *detachments* of eight men each.

The sections are designated according to their actual positions in line, as the *right*, the *centre*, and the *left* sections. If there are four, they are designated according to actual position, as the *right*, the *right-centre*, the *left-centre*, and the *left sections*.

When the company consists of four sections, the right and right-centre sections constitute the right division; the left and left-centre sections, the left division.

None of the designations of the platoons in a section, nor of sections and divisions in the company, are permanent. They shift from one to the other, according to the actual positions of the subdivisions with reference to each other.

Posts of the Officers, Non-Commissioned Officers, etc.

Figures 73 and 74. The captain commanding goes wherever his presence may be necessary or his commands best heard. His position is, in the *order in line*, four yards in front of the centre of the company; in the *order in column*, or when *faced by a flank*, four yards outside the marching flank, opposite the centre of the company.

The lieutenants commanding sections, *in line* or *in column of sections*, are *two* yards in front of the centres of their respective sections; *in columns of platoons* or *of detachments*, or *when faced by a flank*, they are *two* yards outside the marching flank, and opposite the centres of their respective sections; except that, when *faced by a flank*, the chief of the leading section takes his place at the side of the leading file.

In column of divisions, the ranking chief of section in each division is *four* yards in front of the centre of his division; the other chief of section keeps his position of *two* yards in front of the centre of his section.

The lieutenant, chief of caissons, is, *in line, four* yards behind the centre of the company; *in column*, or *faced by a flank*, he is *four* yards outside of the pivot flank, and opposite the centre of the company.

The sergeants, chiefs of pieces, when *in line, in column of sections*, or *faced by a flank*, are on the right of the gun detachments of their respective platoons, in the front rank. *In column of platoons, or of detachments*, they are *one* yard in front of the centre of their platoons or of their gun detachments.

The corporals, gunners, when *in line*, or *column of sections*, are *one* yard behind the right files of their respective gun detachments. In columns of platoons, or detachments, they are on the right of the gun detachments. When the column has a detachment, other than the gun detachment, at its head, the gunner of the platoon to which it belongs will place himself *one* yard in front of its centre, unless the chief of caisson of that piece is acting as its file-closer; in which case the latter leads the column. When *faced by a flank*, they face with the company, and keep their relative positions.

The corporals, chiefs of caissons, are in their places in the ranks as Nos. 8 of the gun detachments, or as the front rank men on the left of their platoons, or they may be assigned as gunners to detachments, other than the gun detachments, in the case already provided for, to prevent the formation of incomplete detachments.

The first sergeant, *in line*, is on the right of the company, in a line with the front rank, and *one* yard from it; *in column*, he is on the marching flank, *one* yard outside the section, or other subdivision, nearest to him when in line. When *faced by a flank*, he faces with the company.

The quartermaster-sergeant occupies positions on the left of the company, corresponding to those of the first sergeant on the right, whether *in line*, *in column*, or *faced by a flank*.

The buglers or trumpeters, *in line*, are on the right of the first sergeant, in one rank, and *two* yards from him; *in column*, they are *six* yards in front or rear of the subdivision next them in line, according as that subdivision forms the head or rear of the column. When the company faces *by flank* they face with it.

The artificers occupy positions on the left of the company corresponding to those of the musicians on the right, whether *in line*, *in column*, or *faced by a flank*.

The guidon forms with the musicians, and on their left, or takes such position as the captain may prescribe.

When, in the movements or manœuvres, the subdivisions originally on the right and left become those of the left and right, the non-commissioned staff, musicians, and artificers remain with the subdivisions near which they were originally formed, and take corresponding positions in line, etc.

APPENDIX.

WAR ORGANIZATION OF A MOUNTED BATTERY OF FOUR AND SIX GUNS.

	4 Pieces.			6 Pieces.			
	OFF'RS.	MEN.	HORSES.	OFF'RS.	MEN.	HORSES.	
Captains......	1	..	..	1	..	..	
Lieutenants...	3	..	..	4	..	..	Chiefs of Sections and Caissons.
Staff Sergeants	..	2	2	..	2	2	Sergeant-Major, or 1st Serg't and Quartermaster-Serg't.
Sergeants.....	..	4	4	..	6	6	Chiefs of Pieces.
Corporals.....	..	8	..	..	12	..	Gunners and Chiefs of Caissons.
Guidons......	..	1	1	..	1	1	
Artificers....	..	*4	4	..	*6	6	
Buglers	..	2	2	..	2	2	
Drivers.......	..	40	60	..	52	84	By order Adjt. and Inspector-Gen'l, No. 81 (Nov. 1, 1862), the number of privates is from 65 to 125—the number of enlisted men should be not less than 25 to each gun, i. e., 100 for a four-gun, and 150 for a six-gun battery.
Cannoneers ...	..	40	..	..	70	..	
Spare	..	..	8	..	..	10	
Total.......	4	101	81	5	151	111	

* By order Adjutant and Inspector-General, No. 81 (November 1, 1862), only 2 artificers for any battery allowed—*entirely insufficient*.

NUMBER AND APPLICATION OF HORSES REQUIRED FOR A MOUNTED BATTERY OF FOUR AND SIX GUNS.

	4 Pieces.	6 Pieces.
Draught. { Battery of Manœuvre.......	48	72
Forge	6	6
Battery Wagon..............	6	6
Spare additional, 1-12.................	5	7
Sergeants'............................	6	8
Artificers'............................	4*	6*
Buglers'.............................	2	2
Guidon's.............................	1	1
Spare................................	3	3
Total..........................	81	111

* Only 2 artificers at present allowed by order No. 81, Adjutant and Inspector-General.

Description of Artillery Horses, and How to Preserve them.

They should be well broken, perfectly sound, with full chests, broad shoulders, short coupled with full barrels, able to move by their weight on the collar say from one thousand thirteen hundred pounds, deep loins, full hind quarters—in other words, active, pony-built, compact horses, not less than five, nor more than ten years old, and from fifteen and a half to sixteen hands high. Narrow chested, long legged, long bodied, and vicious horses are unfit for artillery purposes. They should not be required to pull more than seven hundred pounds to the horse.

The free use of the wisp, brush, and curry-comb, regularly applied, twice daily, for at least thirty minutes, will, with even a short allowance of food, do more toward keeping a horse in good order than full feeding without. A folded blanket, or a moss blanket, adapting itself to the shape of the saddle and condition of the horse, is the best preventive of sore backs. When warm, they should not be watered until rubbed dry, and from buckets rather than from a stream, and never from a well, without allowing the water to stand, and then give a few swallows at a time. If it can be had, give a quart of meal with a little salt to the bucket of water.

The following directions as to grooming, taken from a work by a Board of United States artillery officers, have been found to be full and complete :

"The wisp is to be used when the horse comes in warm from exercise, and the horse is rubbed until dry, from his hind quarters, against the hair, up to his head.

"The curry-comb is used when the horse is dry, beginning always on the near side at the hind quarters, its application being in proportion to the length and foulness of the coat; that is, if the coat is close, being full of dust, and very filthy, use it freely to loosen the coat or the sweat that is dried fast on the skin and roots of the hair, appearing like a white, saltish dust. In the spring the curry-comb should, while the coat is changing, be used judiciously, as a removal of the hair too rapidly exposes the horse to the sudden changes of temperature. Proceeding from the hind quarters, descend to the quarters, minding not to scratch or injure the horse. The legs below the houghs are not to be touched with the curry-comb, unless the dirt is matted on the joints of the hough, which may be carefully loosened with the curry-comb. The comb works unpleasantly on that part, and must be handled lightly. Next proceed to the fetlocks, back, loins, flank, belly, shoulders, arms, chest, and neck, omitting no part that the curry-comb can be conveniently applied to; but tender places, thin of hair, or rubbed by the harness, need not be touched; they should be rubbed with the wisp; observe, therefore, to begin with the curry-comb on the near hind quarters and finish with the head, keeping the comb in the right hand. After currying the near side, proceed with the opposite side; here use the left hand; this done, wisp off those places not touched by the curry-comb; then use the brush. Begin first at the head on the near side, taking the brush in the left hand and the curry-comb in the right, brushing more particularly those parts where the dust is more apt to lodge, proceed down the neck; the scurf of the neck, next the head, and the scrag next the mane are difficult to clean. Apply the brush backward and forward on these places, finishing by leaving the coat smooth, clear the brush from dust after every two or three strokes with the curry-comb; proceed in the reverse order used by the curry-comb, taking in those parts not touched by the curry-comb, viz: under the chest between the forelegs, the inside of the elbow or arm, and the parts about the fetlocks—the skin under the flank and the hind quarters must be free from dust, soft, and so clean as not to soil a white cloth. The curry-comb begins at the hind quarters and ends at the head.

"The brush begins at the head, and, taking in all parts of the horse, ends at the quarters. Horses should always be groomed at the picket-rope, unless in very stormy weather. After grooming, the chief of each piece inspects his horses, exacting that the rules relating to grooming shall have been obeyed—if passed by the sergeant, then the horses of each piece to be led up successively to the battery officer of the day for inspection. Any horse not passed by him should be taken back to the picket-rope, and the driver made to groom him double the usual time in the presence of the sergeant of the piece. A chest of boxes of thin, light wood may be carried strapped on the foot-boards."

Further directions for the care and preservation of horses will be found in the standing orders to Andrews' Artillery Battalion.

Great care should be given to the fitting of collars and saddles. A pad or piece of sheepskin should be used near the spot rubbed. By using a folded blanket, or moss blanket, and by *proper riding*, sore backs should be a rare occurrence. By a solution of alum-water, the necks and backs may be rendered tough. Relieving them from work, castile soap and wet cloths, with cold water, will soon effect a cure if prompt attention be given in the beginning. Collars should be kept soft and supple by cleaning, oiling, airing, and beating them. Neatsfoot oil is decidedly the best; melted lard when neatsfoot oil can not be had.

HEAD-QUARTERS, ANDREWS' BATTALION ARTILLERY,
Milford Station, March 31, 1863.

Standing Orders to be rigidly enforced by company officers of batteries, who will be held responsible by their battalion commander.

Roll Calls — Reveille. — Reveille will be blown, until further orders, at a quarter before six, and roll called at six precisely; commissioned officers and all enlisted men are required to be present, save the following: *The battery officer of the day* (who must visit the guard at least once between midnight and daylight, and not divest himself of his clothing), and those on guard during the night.

Sick Calls will be blown at half-past seven o'clock, at battalion head-quarters; at eight o'clock, the first sergeant will be present at head-quarters with men able to attend, with a list signed by officer in command of company, and by himself, of *all persons* absent from calls of preceding day and reveille call.

Retreat will be blown at a quarter before six, and roll called at six o'clock — at least one commissioned officer and all enlisted men are required to be present.

Taps will be blown at nine o'clock, at which time all officers and enlisted men must be in quarters.

Drill Calls. — The time for drill call may be selected by officers commanding company; they must drill at least *two hours* each day from the time of assembling, and the officer commanding battery will notify battalion commander as to the hours selected—at least one commissioned officer will be present at every drill, and see that the non-commissioned officers properly instruct the men.

Feeding, Watering, and Grooming.—Grain will be fed twice daily, long food at night; sergeants, with drivers, will go from reveille roll call directly to the stables, and feed. After feeding, the horses will be led to the picket-rope and thoroughly groomed. Great care must be given to rub the legs, joints, and under the fetlocks dry, to avoid scratches, and grease heel—captain and other officers must be present, except the battery officer of preceding day—then taken to and from water in a walk by twos in column, accompanied by the battery officer of the day. After grooming, the stables will be cleaned by a detail for the purpose, under charge of the battery officer of the day. At four o'clock stable call shall be blown, when the horses will be taken to and from water by twos in column, accompanied by the battery officer of the day, then thoroughly groomed and then fed; each time they must be groomed at least *thirty minutes* to each horse, and then inspected by the battery officer. If not properly groomed, he will cause the driver, under the direction of his sergeant, to immediately groom the horse *double* the usual time, and then be brought to him for inspection.

Harness.—Racks must be placed for harness whenever one day's halt is made; at other times, it may be placed on foot-boards and tongues of carriages, *never on the ground*—care must be taken to keep the harness in *good repair*, well greased with neatsfoot oil, and cleaned.

Horses shall not be tied at any time to the guns or caissons. A light picket-rope (1-inch) can be carried on caisson of No. 1 gun. Men kicking, or striking with buts of whips their horses, must be severely punished, and each case reported *at once*, with character of person and punishment to the battalion commander. Baggage must not be placed on limbers or caissons. Cooking utensils and blankets must be carried on the company wagon, also knapsacks, or on the backs of men; none of these articles shall be carried on limbers or caissons. No lounging or careless riding to be allowed, and drivers to be required to dismount at halts on marches. When artillery is marching with infantry, no watering must be allowed on the march. Pole props not to be allowed to hang loose, but to be placed when halted. Ammunition when expended to be *without delay* replaced by requisition on ordnance officer. To be carefully sunned daily when practicable, and any defective ammunition to be at once reported in writing. After an action, a report to be at once made, giving full particulars as to the number of rounds fired, also the number of men and horses killed and wounded, together with the names of any commissioned officers or enlisted men who shall have been conspicuous for gallantry or the reverse. It will not always be possible in a campaign to observe the hours appointed, or literally obey some of the duties enjoined. But the spirit of them must be obeyed. It is expected that commissoned and non-commissioned officers shall make themselves thoroughly conversant with their duties, and, as far as practicable, with those of grade next above them.

HEAD-QUARTERS DEPARTMENT NORTHERN VIRGINIA,
April 4, 1863.

SPECIAL ORDER,}
No. 94.   }

[Extract.]

VIII....A board, to consist of Colonel S. Crutchfield, Lieutenant-Colonel R. Snowden Andrews, and Major H. P. Jones, is hereby appointed to meet at the camp of the artillery of the 2d corps on the 10th instant, or as soon thereafter as practicable, to express an opinion as to the proper proportion of projectiles to accompany the 12-pounder Napoleon, the 10-pounder Parrott, and 3-inch Rifle guns; also, whether the efficiency of artillery will be impaired by omitting the prolonge with the gun-carriage, and extra wheel and axle with the caisson.

By command of General LEE.

W. W. TAYLOR,
A. A. General.

REPORT OF BOARD OF ARTILLERY OFFICERS CONVENED BY VIRTUE OF SPECIAL ORDER, No. 94, HEAD-QUARTERS A. N. V., APRIL 4, 1863.

Head-quarters Artillery 2d Corps, April 10, 1863.

The board met at one o'clock, P. M., pursuant to Special Order, No. 94, Head-quarters A. N. V., current series. After due consideration of the several questions therein submitted to us, we have the honor to submit the following report:

1. We deem it decidedly inexpedient to abandon the *prolonge* on gun-carriages. It is light in weight, while experience has shown it exceedingly valuable in a campaign—indeed, almost indispensable. It has several times happened during the past year, in this command, that the pintle-hook on the gun-limber has given away, and then the gun was carried by bending a pole over the limber and lashing to it with the prolonge the lunette. Without this resource the gun or its caisson, one would have been abandoned of necessity. Again, the prolonge has been found invaluable in hauling the gun up steep declivities and through very bad roads.

2. We also deem it inexpedient to give up the fifth wheel on the caissons. It is very heavy, and much increases the draft, but spare wheels are always needed after a battle; and, in dry weather, on hard roads, it is very often necessary to take off the wheels and cut the tires if circumstances permit, while, if they do not, some of the wheels give way entirely, and these fifth wheels are the only resource in the case.

3. We believe that the best proportion for the several kinds of ammunition for 12-pounder Napoleon guns is as follows: In each ammunition-chest, eight rounds solid shot, fixed; sixteen rounds spherical-case shot, fixed; four rounds shell, fixed; and three rounds canister, fixed. And then we would recommend that there be made for each gun eight rounds of canister, thus: The tin canister to be of the present size, and, instead of being charged with the twenty-seven ordi-

nary iron shot, to be filled with round musket-bullets of calibre 0.69. No cartridges to be attached to or provided for these canister. They are to be carried two in each chest, placed in the farther end of the division appropriated to canister, and sitting one on the top of the other. They are to be used either on top of an ordinary canister, or on a solid shot, at short range, when it is believed they will prove highly efficient. Thus there are really *five* rounds of canister in each chest, three being fixed and two not.

4. Each of the ammunition-chests of the 10-pounder Parrott or 3-inch rifled gun, is capable of carrying sixty rounds of ammunition, so that all four boxes carry two hundred and forty rounds. This we believe to be too much. Two hundred rounds should be enough for one engagement, and one hundred and eighty rounds in the caisson form a load far too heavy for six horses. As it would not be advisable to change the dimensions of these boxes, we recommend that the four shall carry only two hundred and four rounds. And to dispose the load as advantageously as possible that this reduction of thirty-six rounds be made in the rear chest of the caisson, while the divisions thus left vacant be devoted to carrying fuze-ignitors, except of course the number necessary to be carried in the gun-limber box for use with the gun, should it become separated from its caisson. Thus the chests on the limbers will be filled to their full capacity of sixty rounds each. So will the middle chest. In each of these chests we recommend that there be carried six rounds of canister, eighteen shells, and thirty-six rounds of shrapnel; while in the rear chest, which carries but thirty-six rounds in all, there should be twenty-four shrapnel and twelve shells,

making a total for each gun of eighteen canisters, one hundred and thirty-two case-shot, and sixty-six shells. We have the honor to remain,

Very respect'y, your ob't serv'ts,

(Signed)   S. CRUTCHFIELD,
Colonel and Chief Artillery 2d Corps.

(Signed)   R. SNOWDEN ANDREWS,*
Lieutenant-Colonel commanding Battalion Artillery.

(Signed)   H. P. JONES,
Major commanding Battalion Artillery.

Major TAYLOR,
A. A. General.

---

* I do not concur with the other members of the board in regard to the fifth wheel on the caissons. I respectfully recommend that only the alternate caissons shall carry a fifth wheel. This will give two spare wheels to each four-gun battery, and eight to a battalion, sufficient in my judgment to meet any ordinary emergency. Weak or disabled teams can be thus relieved, and entire teams kept from breaking down. The horses of the caissons have always suffered more than those of the guns. The weights of caisson and gun, light 12-pounder, or Napoleon, equipped for field service, differ only forty-six pounds, why, then, should one team suffer more than the other, because from the weight of the rear chest and the spare wheel exercising by their positions a leverage which changes the line of draught very seriously whenever the rear wheels are below the plane of the front—for instance, when in a hole or ascending a hill. The weight of the fifth wheel is one hundred and eighty pounds; at times it exerts by its position, by changing the line of draught, more than the equivalent of five hundred pounds. Believing eight spare wheels to be sufficient for a battalion of four companies, I again respectfully recommend that only the alternate caissons shall carry a fifth wheel.

R. SNOWDEN ANDREWS,
Lieutenant-Colonel commanding Battalion Artillery.

EXPLANATION

OF THE

SIGNS IN THE PLATES.

Piece drawn by six horses			
Caisson drawn by six horses			
Limber drawn by six horses			
Piece in battery			
Gun detachment			
Captain commanding battery			
Lieut. commanding a section			
Chief of the line of caissons			
Chief of piece			
Chief of caisson			
Horse not mounted			
Cannoneer at his post			
Bugler or trumpeter			
Chief of piece dismounted			

– – – – Indicates the front of a line of carriages or of a detachment in an original, intermediate, or final position, or in a change of direction

·········· Indicates an intermediate position

Pl. 2

NAPOLEON GUN,

or 12 Pdr. Light Field Gun, (Bronze.)

SCALE 1/10th

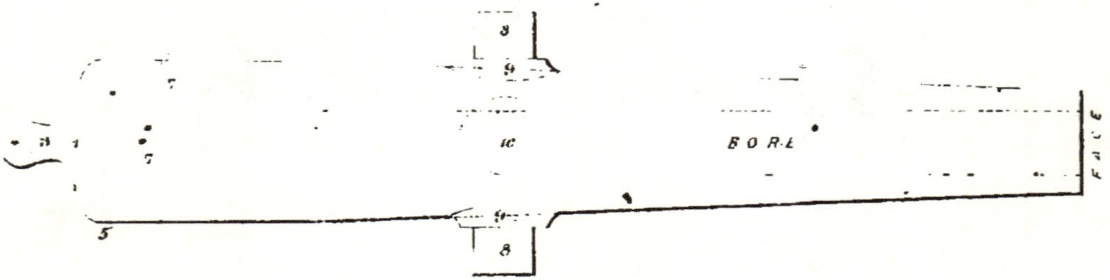

FACE

BORE

Cascable {
1. Base of Breech.
2. Neck.
3. Knob.
4. Baseline.

6. Bottom of Bore.
7. Horizontal & Vertical projection of Vent & vend piece
8. Horizontal projection of Trunnions
9. do Rimbases
10. Vertical projection of Trunnions & Rimbases.

50 inches

PL 3

NAPOLEON GUN,
or 12 Pdr Light Field Gun. (Bronze)

SCALE 1/32

1. Lock chain bolt, & eye plate
2. Pointer Lock chain
3. Sponge & Rammer stops
4. Sponge Stave hasp
5. Earplate for do
6. Earplate to support Worm Key Chain & Key
7. Box of Elevating screw (Brass)
8. Elevating screw (Head & Handles)
9. Washer hook for Handspike
10. do   do   for Lock chain
11. Lunstock Socket.
12. Cap-square chain
13. do-square
14. &c   Key Chain & Key
15. Trunnion plate
16. Handspike ring
17. Sponge hook
18. Axle body (Wheel)
19. Axle tree (Iron)
20. Under strap

9 are also the
10. extremities of
21. The assembling bolts

Stock, Head, invove, Trail, and the rounding of the Trail

22. Large } Pointing Ring
23. Small }

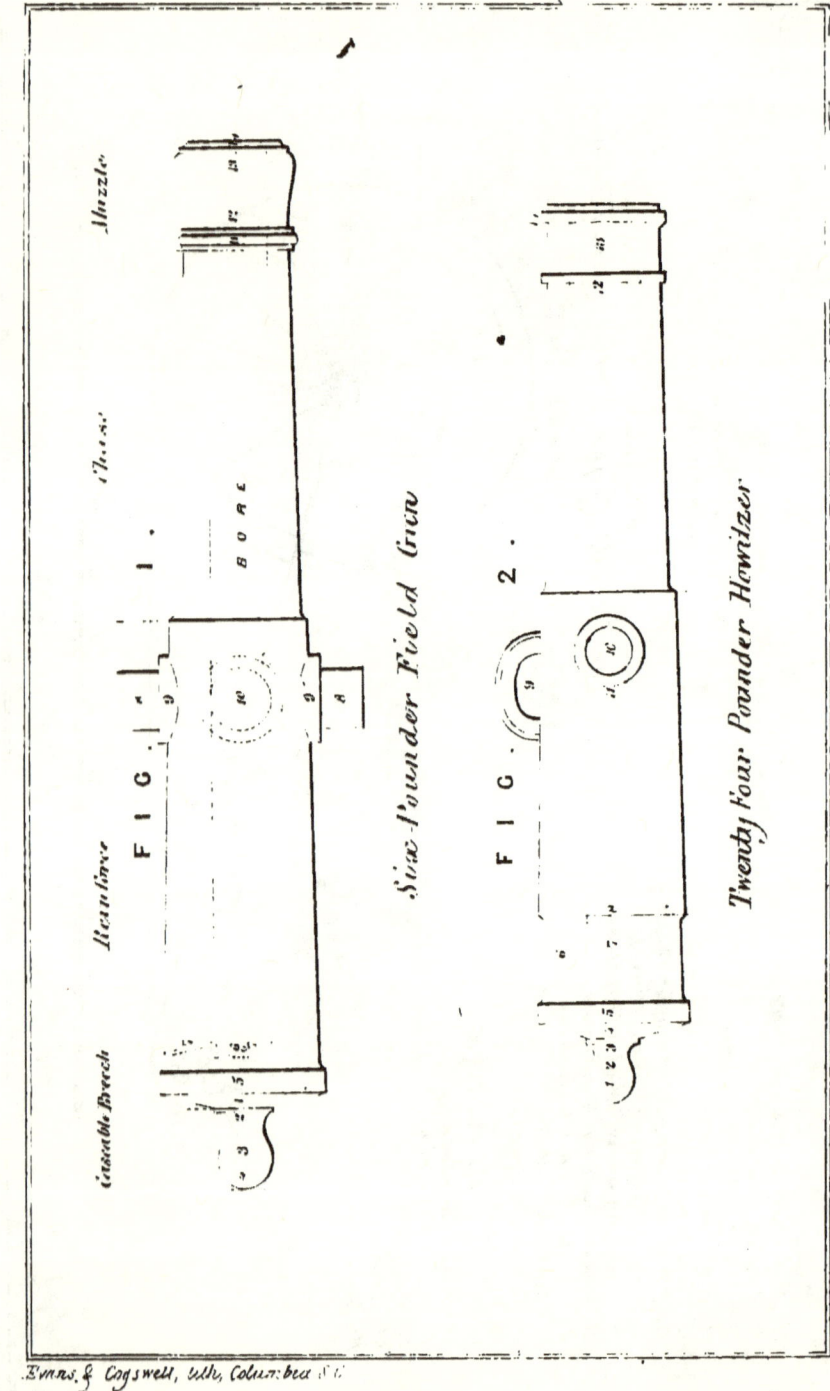

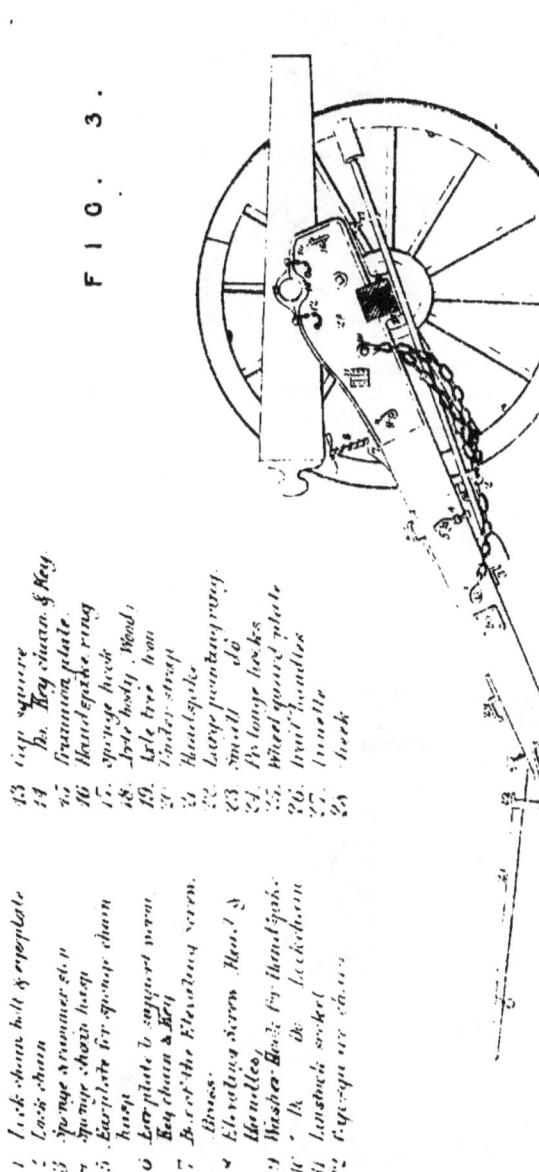

Pl. 5

FIG. 3.

1 Lock chain bolt & eyeplate
2 Lock chain
3 Sponge rammer stop
4 Sponge chain hasp
5 Eyeplate for sponge chain hasp
6 Lockplate to support worm
   Keychain & Key
7 B. of the Elevating screw
   Brass
8 Elevating Screw Head &
   Handles
9 Washer Hooks for thumbpiece
10 D.o D.o Lockchain
11 Lunstock socket
12 Eyepieces for chains

13 Cap square
14 D.o Key chain & Key
15 Trunnion plate
16 Handspike ring
17 Sponge hook
18 Axtr body Wood
19 Axle tree Iron
20 Linch-strap
21 Handspoke
22 Large pointer prog
23 Small do
24 Potenge locks
25 Wheel guard plate
26 Trail handles
27 Lunette
28 Hook

6 pr. Hunter Field Gun & Carriage

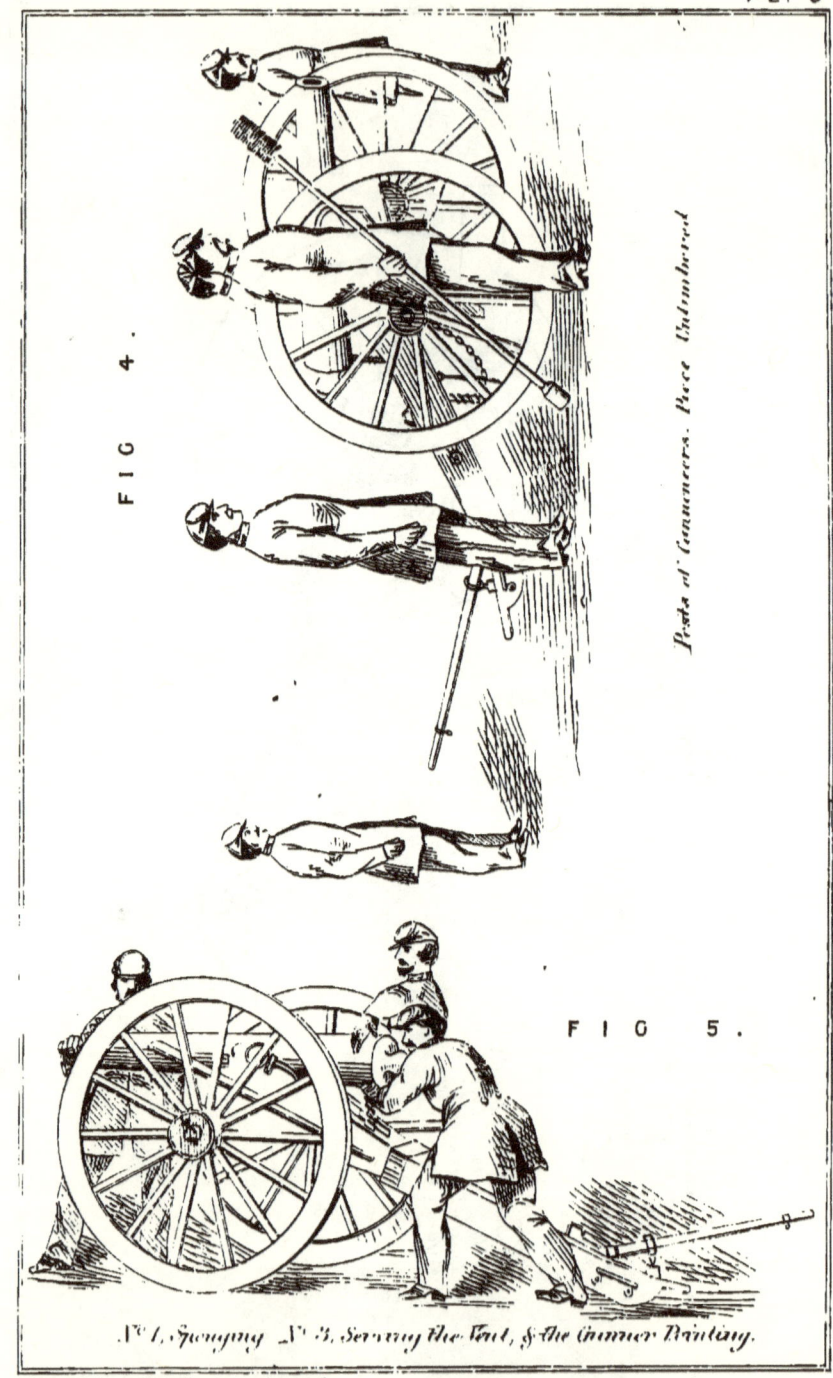

PL 7

First motion of Load

Second motion of Load

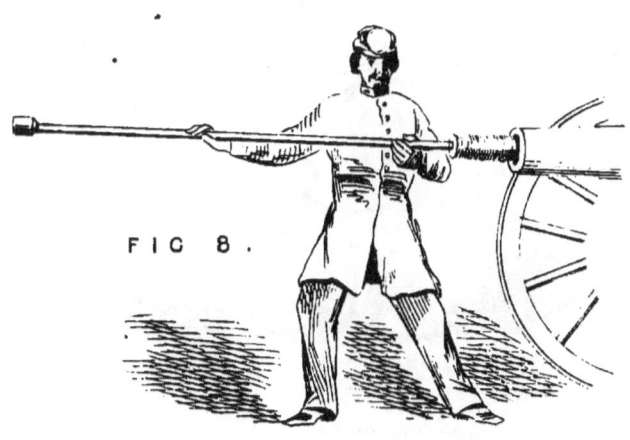

Third motion of Load

Evans & Cogswell, lith, Columbia, S.C.

PL 8

FIG 9.

Fourth motion of Load.

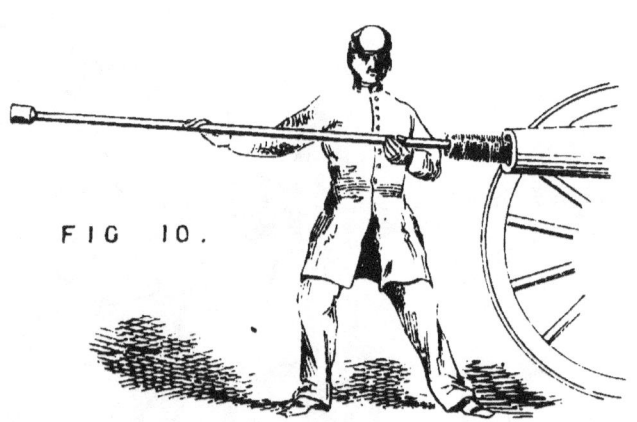

FIG 10.

Second motion of Sponge.

FIG 11.

Third motion of Sponge

FIG 12.

Fourth motion of Sponge

First motion of Ram

Second motion of Ram

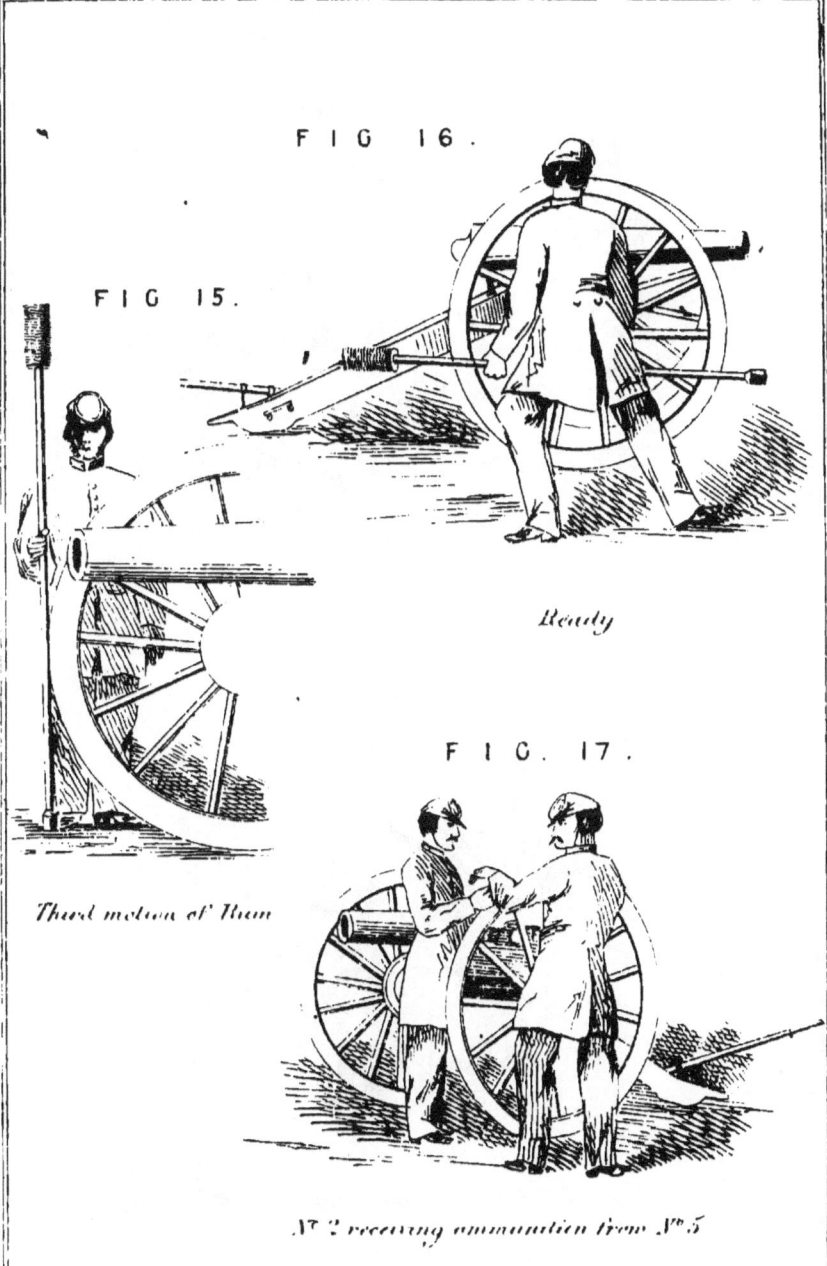

PL 12

FIG. 18.

Ready.

FIG. 19.

N.º 5 delivering ammunition to N.º 2.

Pl. 13

Fig 20. By Hand to the Front. Piece Limbered

Fig 21. Moving the Piece Forward by Hand. Piece Limbered

Evans & Cogswell, Lith. Columbia S.C.

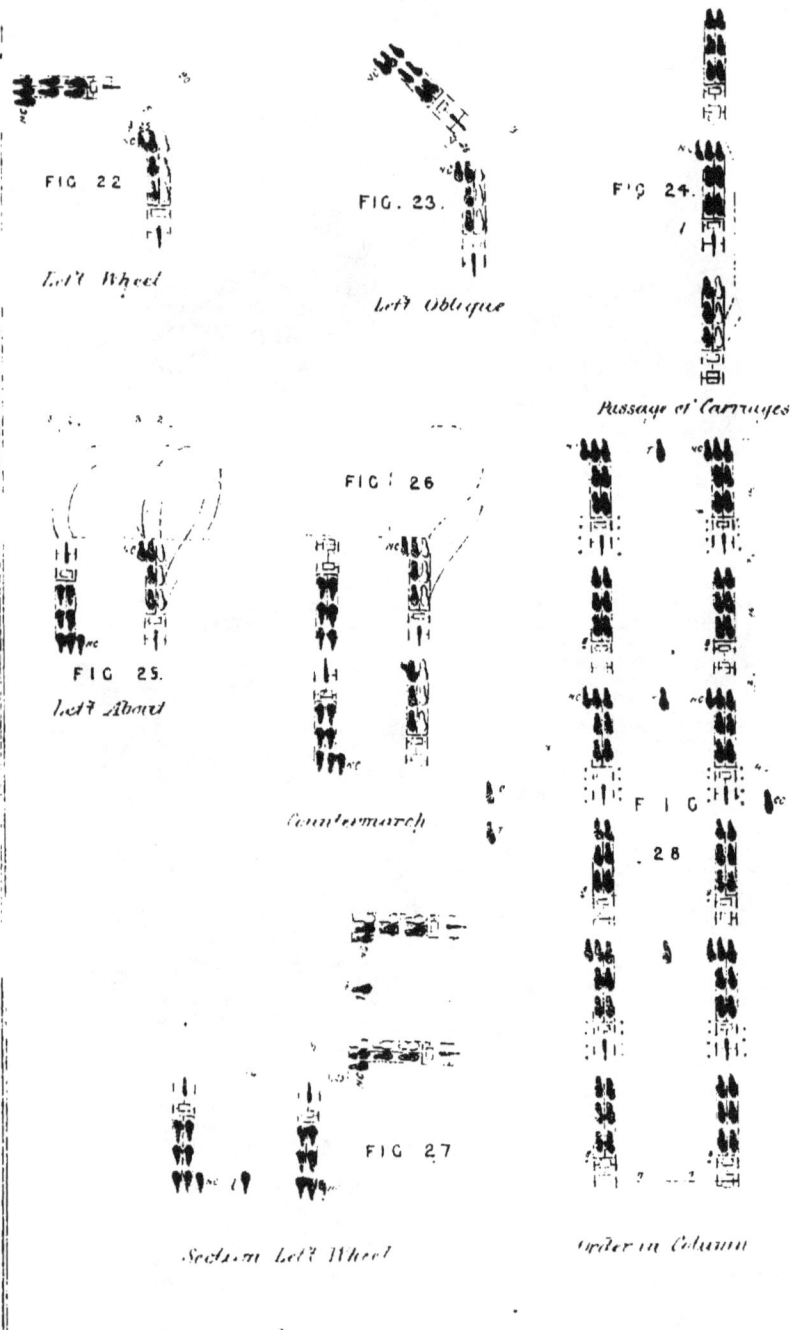

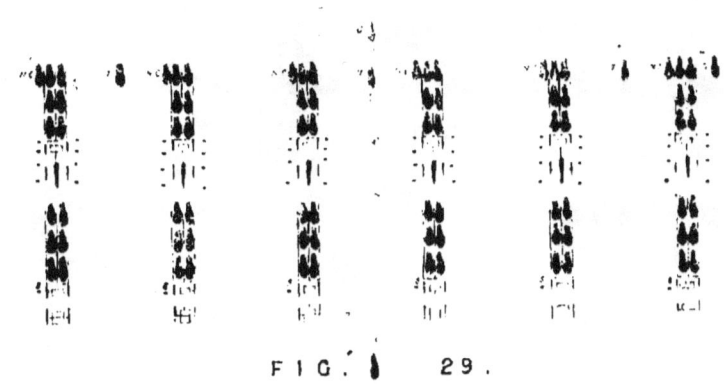

FIG. 29.

Order in Line

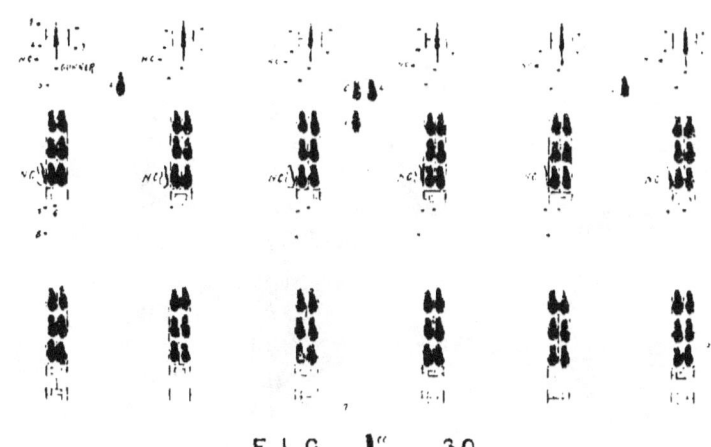

FIG. 30

Order in Battery

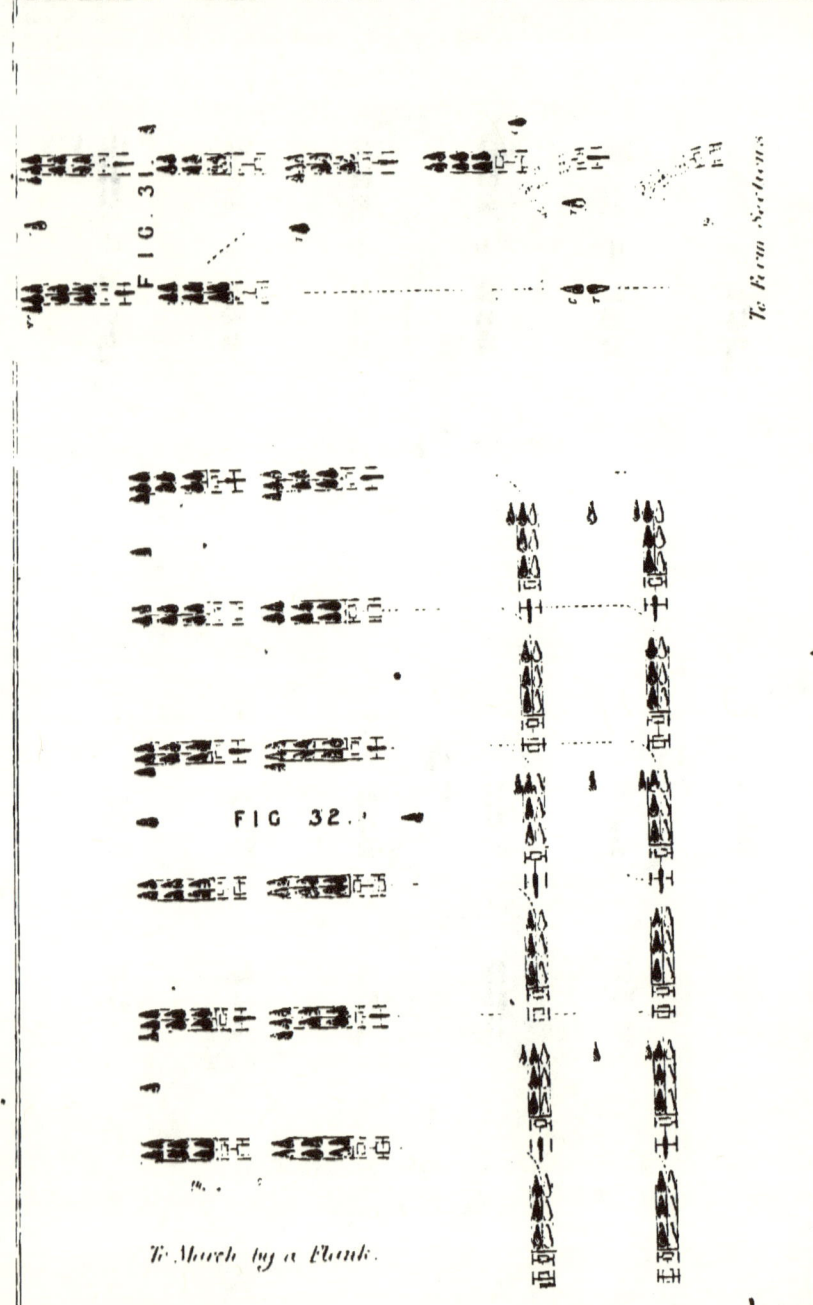

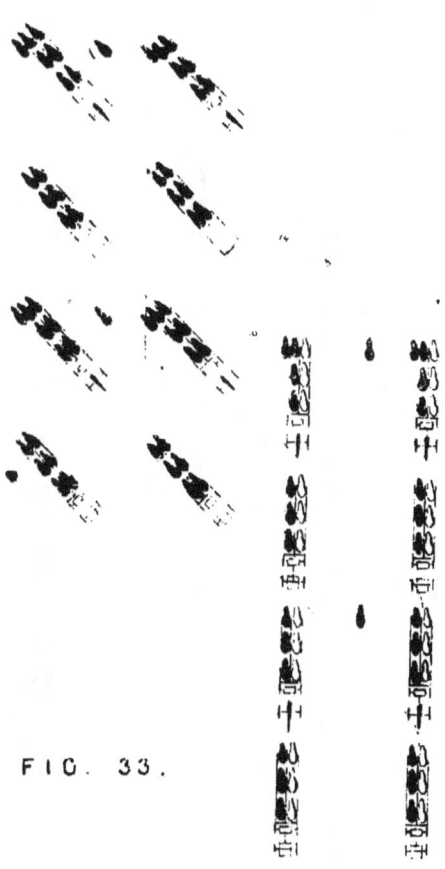

FIG. 33.

Œil Oblique

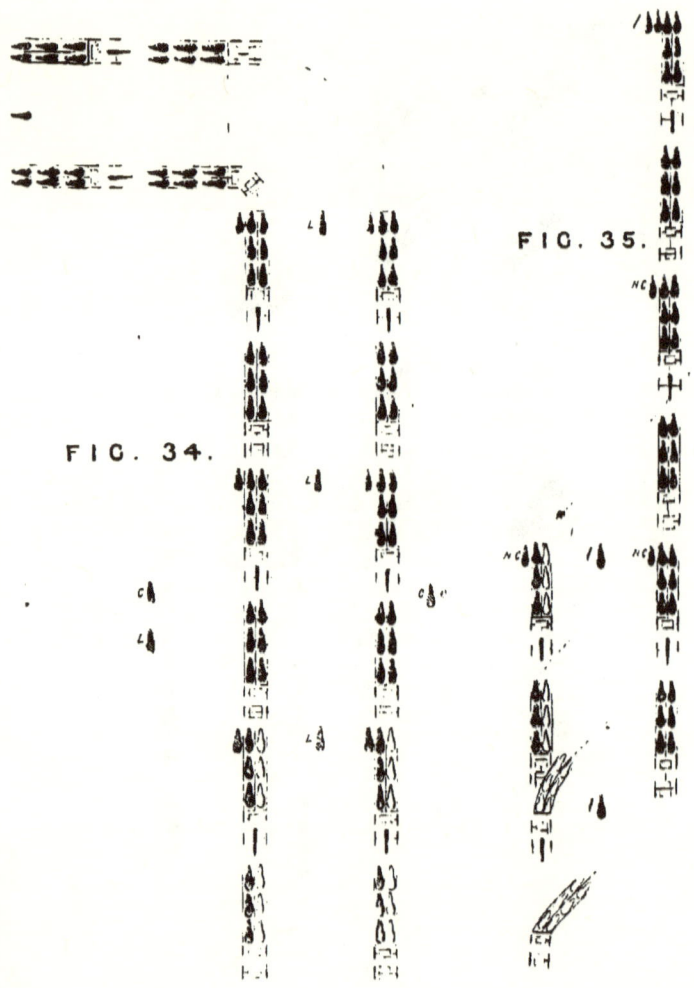

PL. 18

FIG. 34.

FIG. 35.

Head of Column to the Left

By the Right Breah Sections

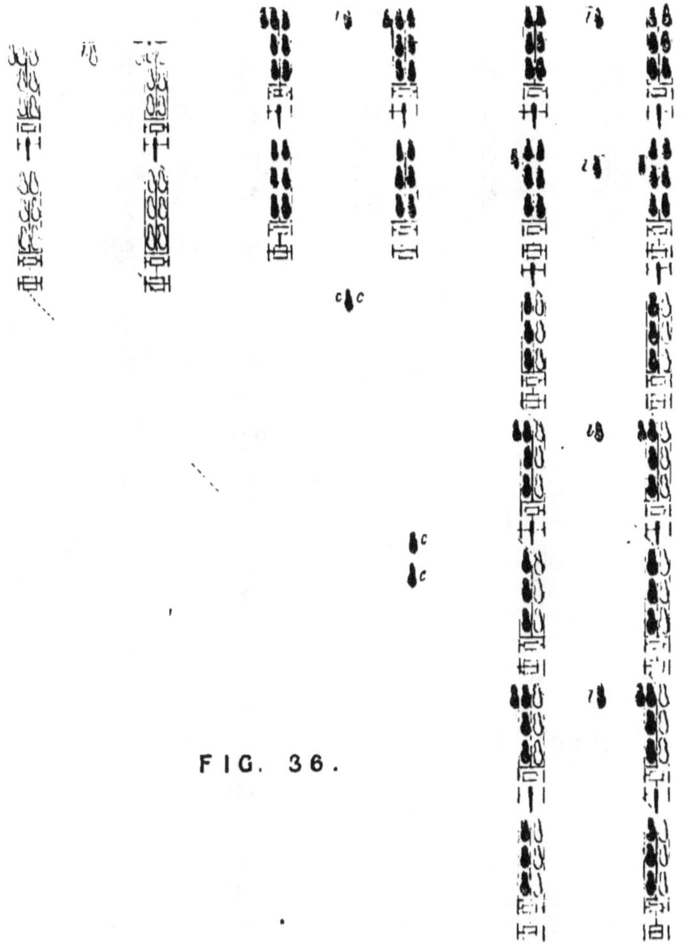

PL. 19

FIG. 36.

Forward into Line.

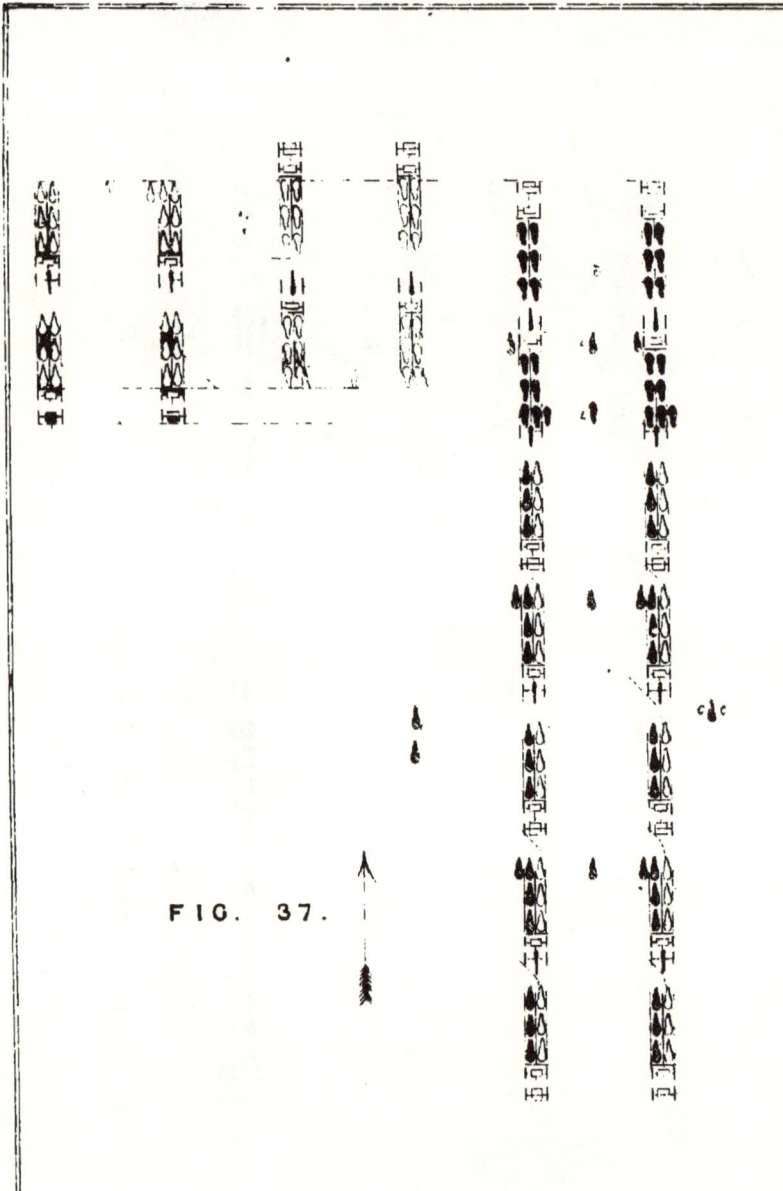

FIG. 37.

Into Line Face to the Rear.

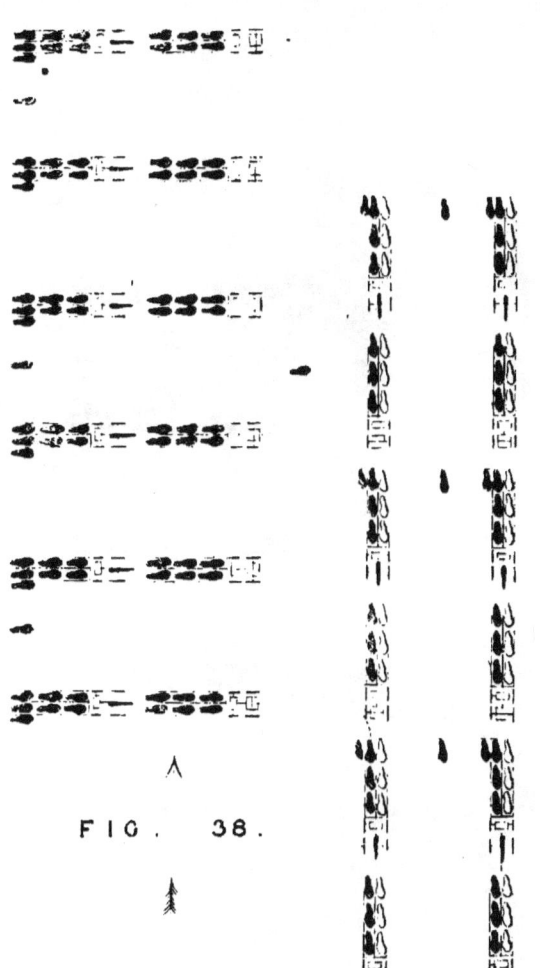

FIG. 38.

To the Left, rifle fire.

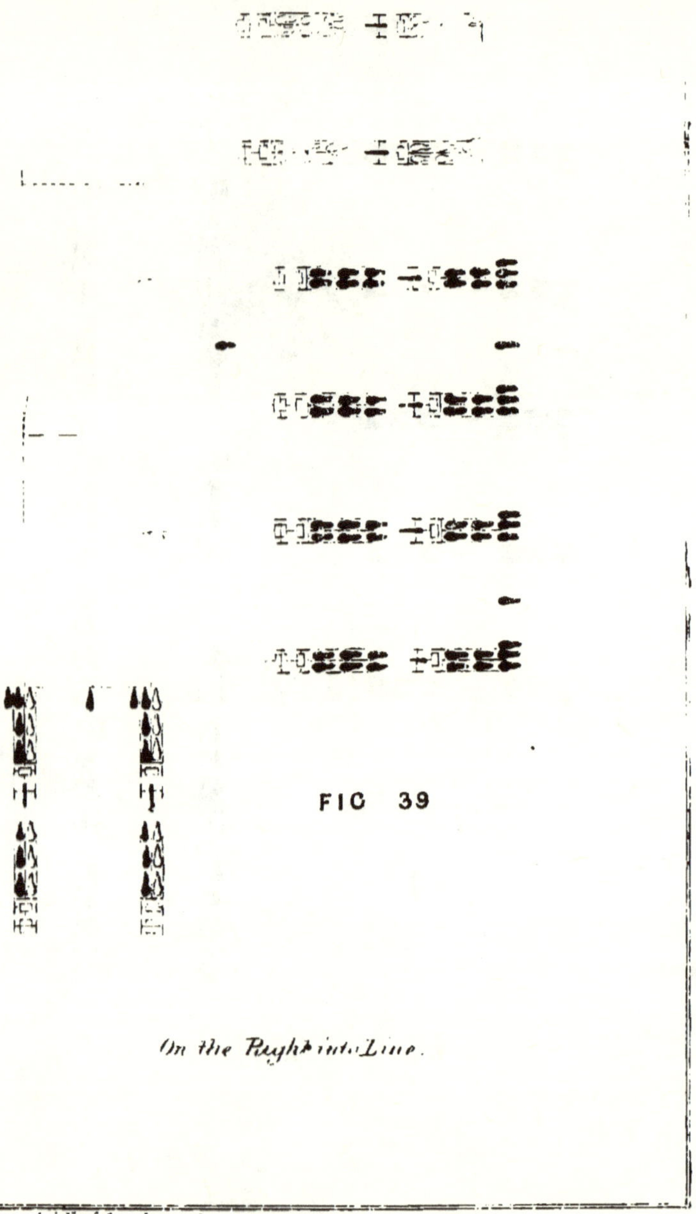

FIG 39

On the Right into Line.

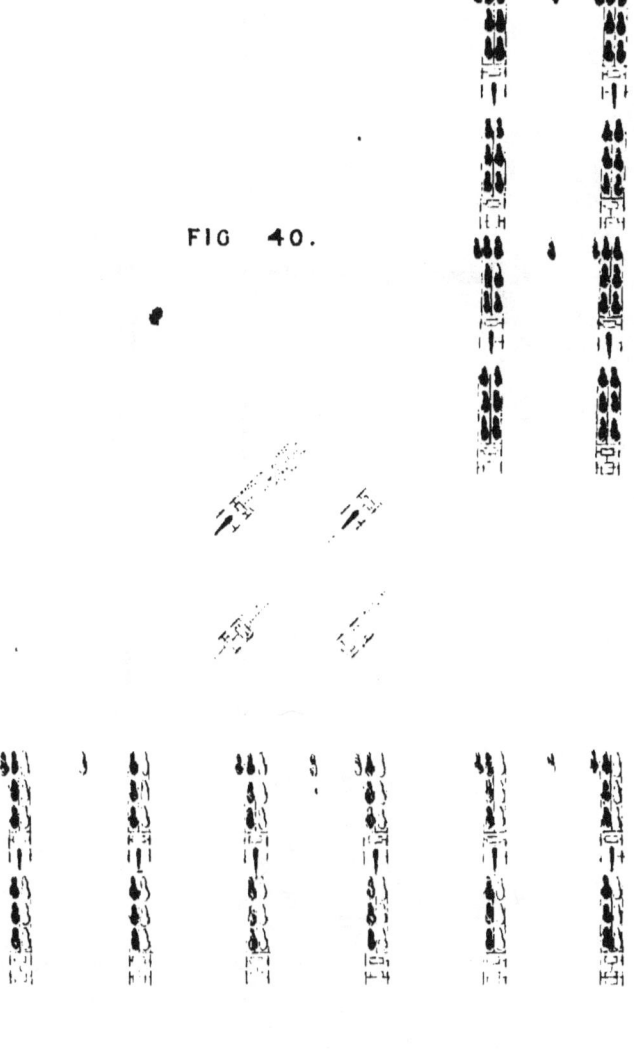

FIG 40.

FIG 41.

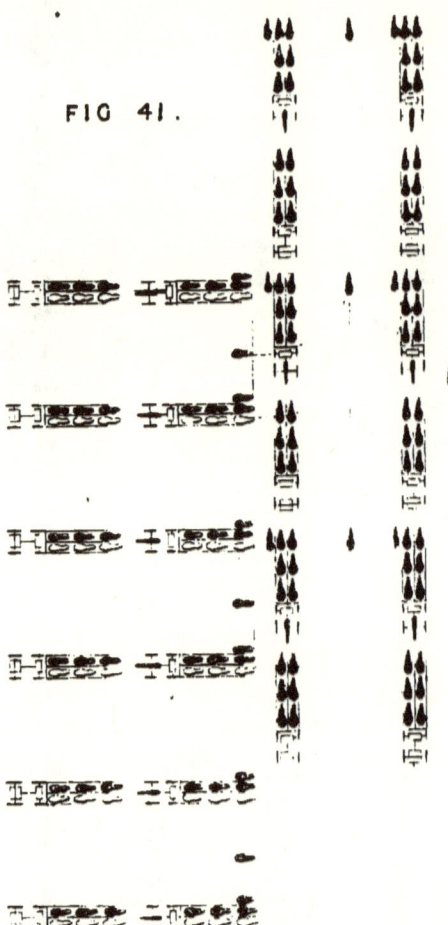

To Break into Column to the Left.

FIG 42.

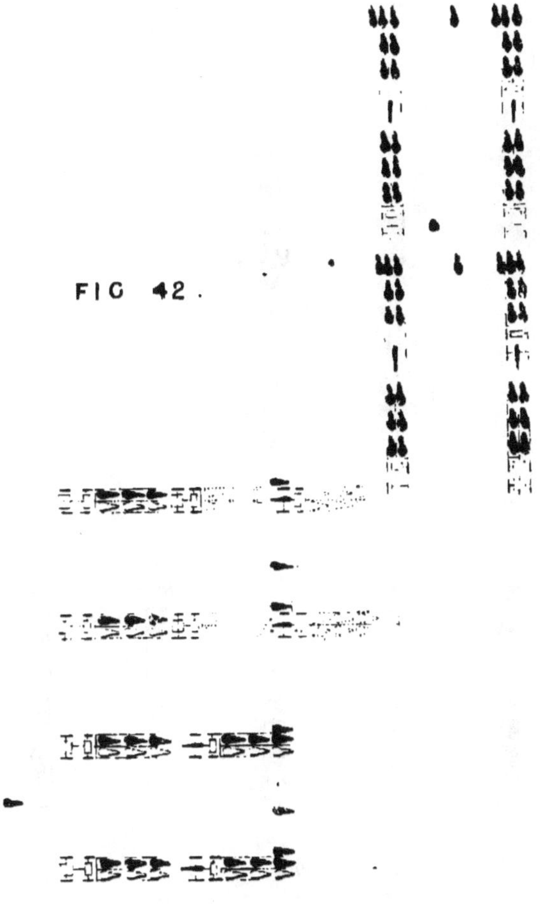

To Break from the Right to march to the Left

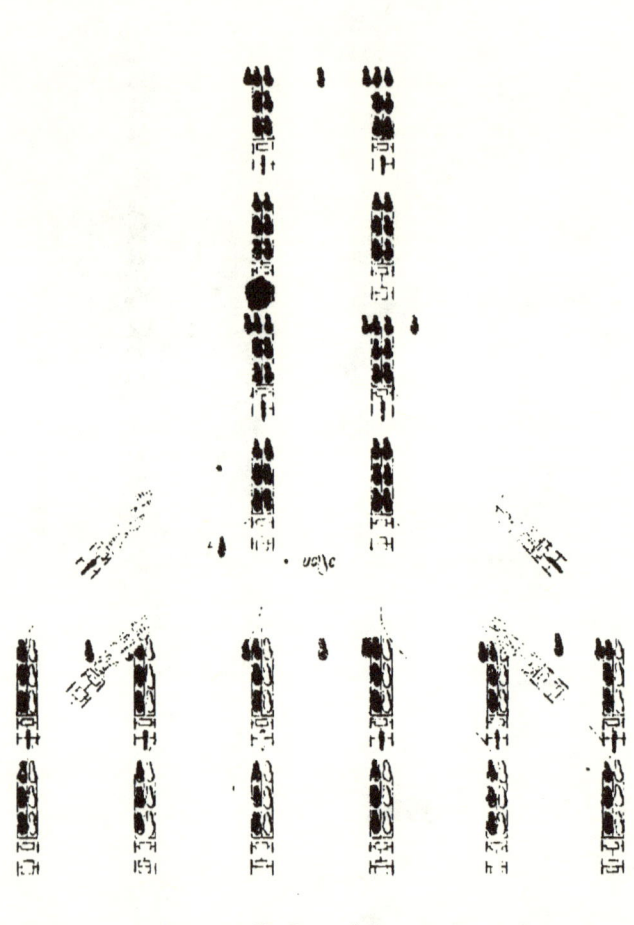

FIG. 43.

To form Double Column.

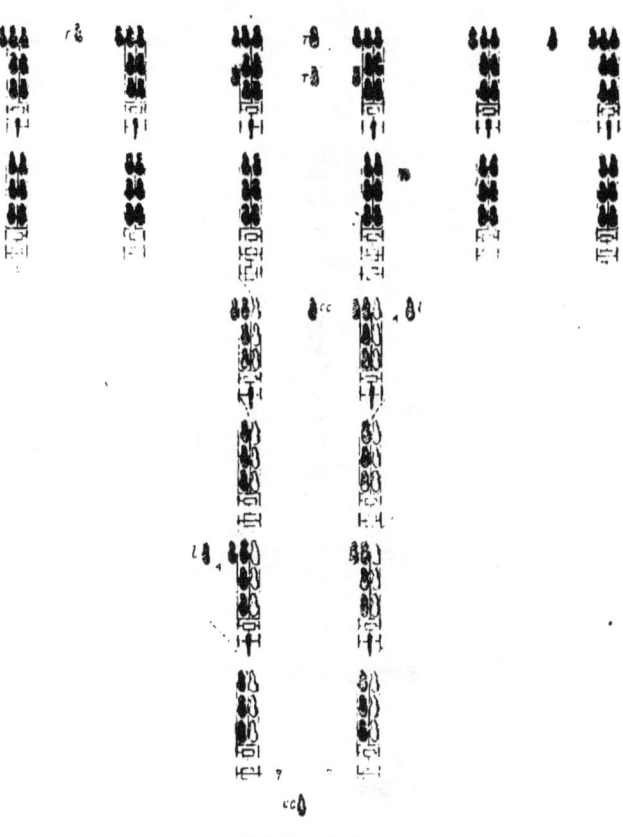

FIG. 44.

To Deploy the Double Column into Line to the Front.

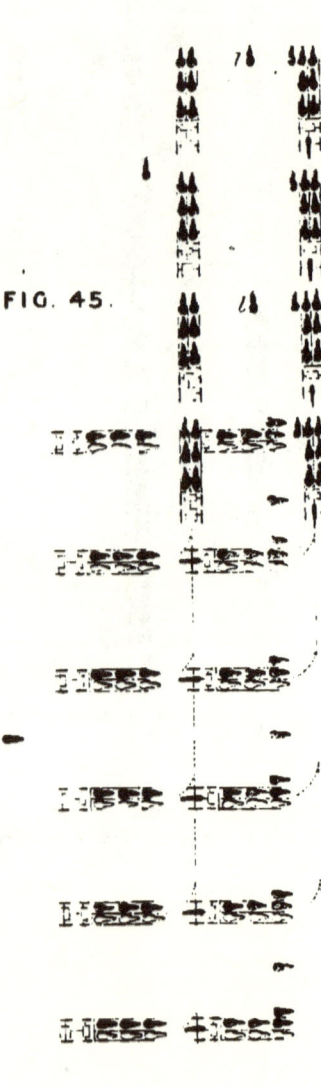

FIG. 45.

Flank March

PL 29

FIG. 46.

The Oblique Mood

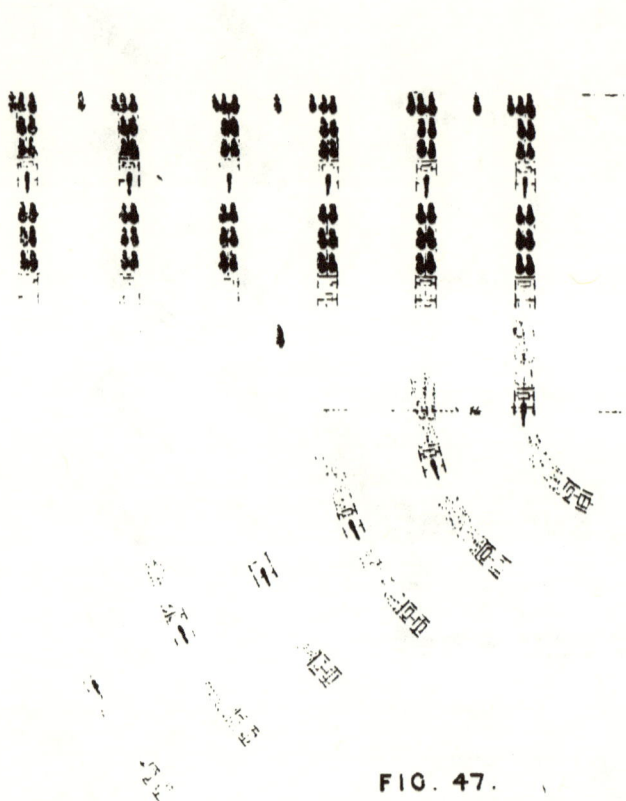

FIG. 47.

Change of Direction in Line

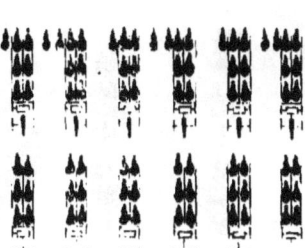

FIG 48.

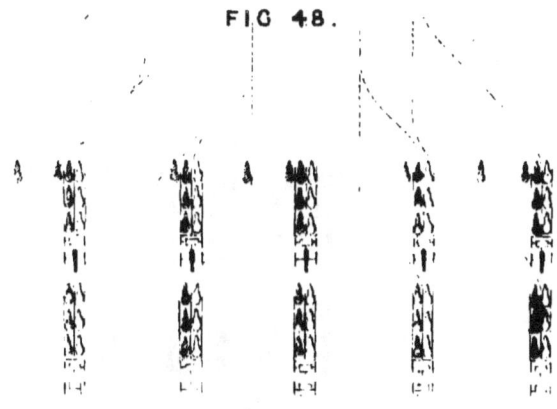

At Close Intervals

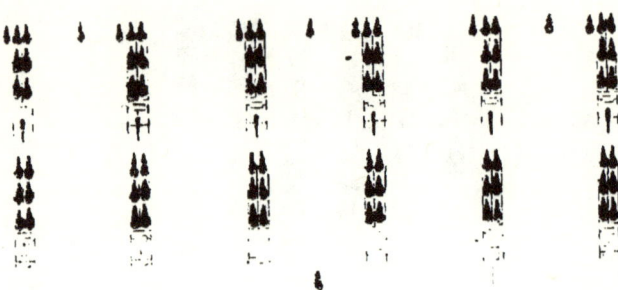

FIG. 49.

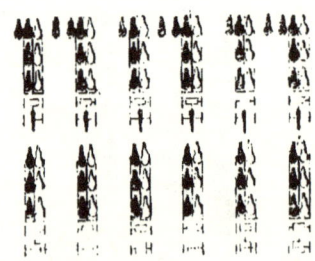

To Resume Intervals

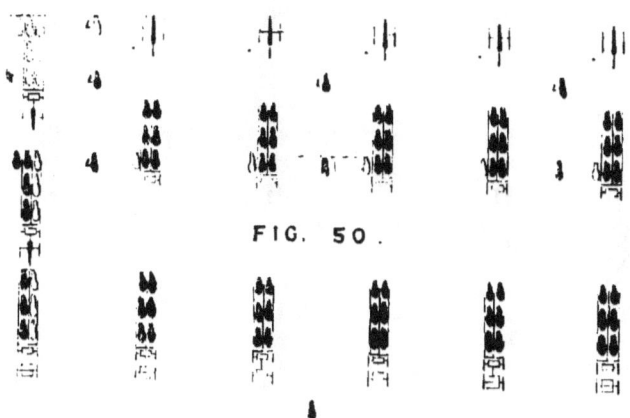

FIG. 50.

In Line with Pieces in Front, to form in Battery to the Front.

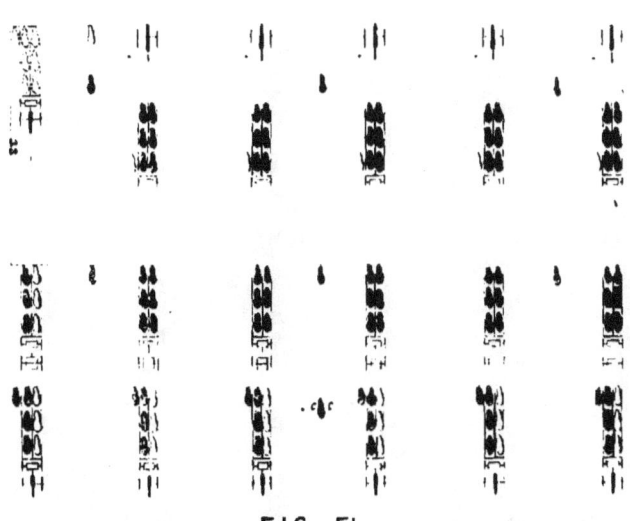

FIG. 51.

In Line with Caissons in Front, to form in Battery to the Front.

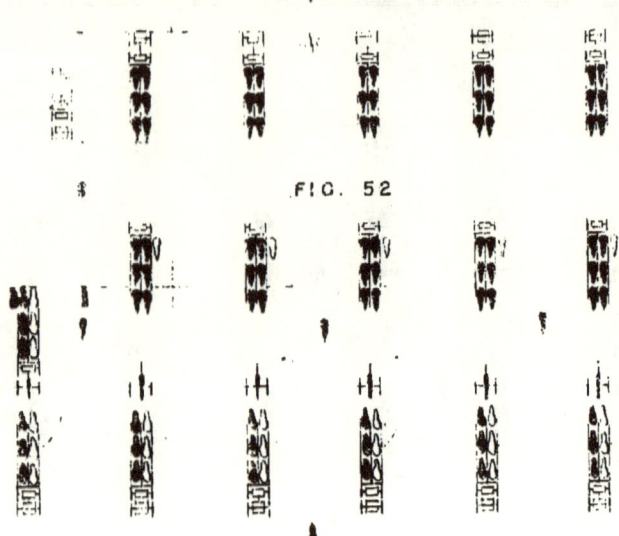

FIG. 52

In Line, with Pieces in Front, to form in Battery to the Rear

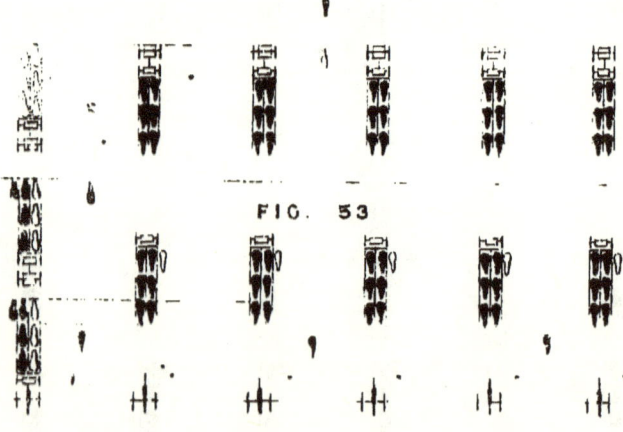

FIG. 53

In Line, with Caissons in Front, to form in Battery to the Rear

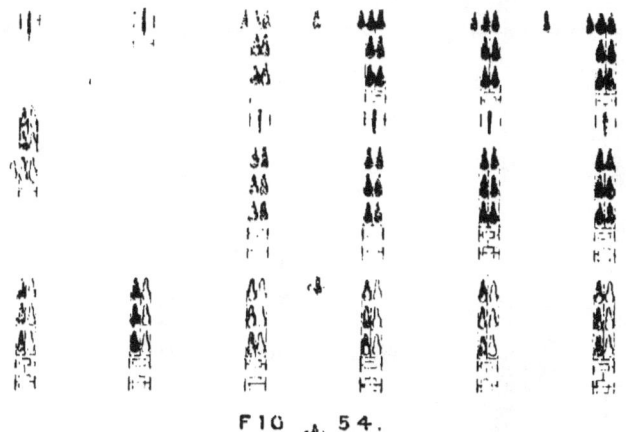

FIG. 54.

In Battery, to form in Line to the Front with Pieces in Front, by limbering to the Rear.

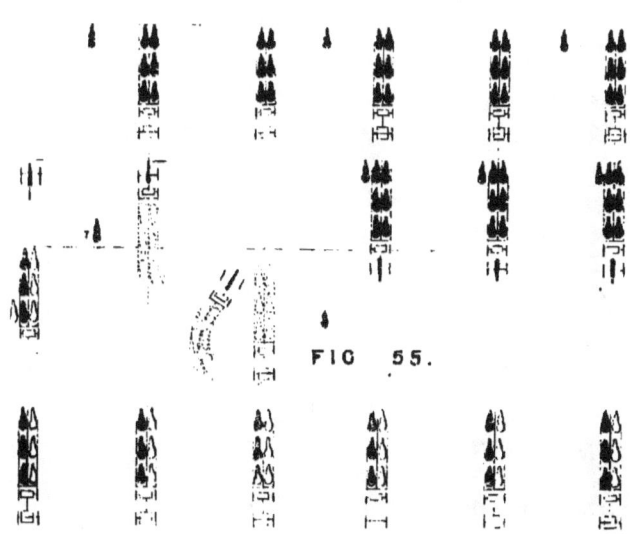

FIG. 55.

In Battery, to form in Line to the Front, with Caissons in Front, by Limbering to the Rear.

PL 36

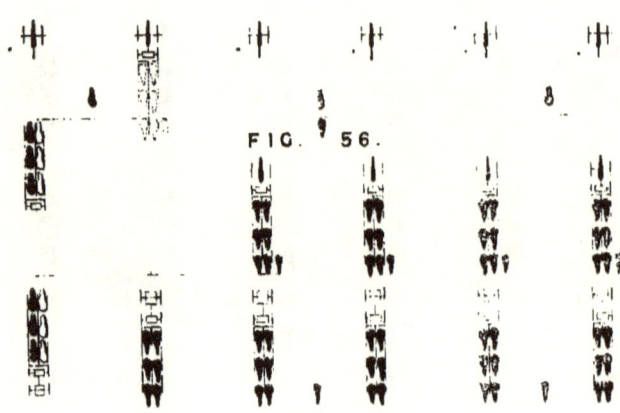

FIG. 56.

In Battery, to form in Line to the Rear, with Caissons in Front.

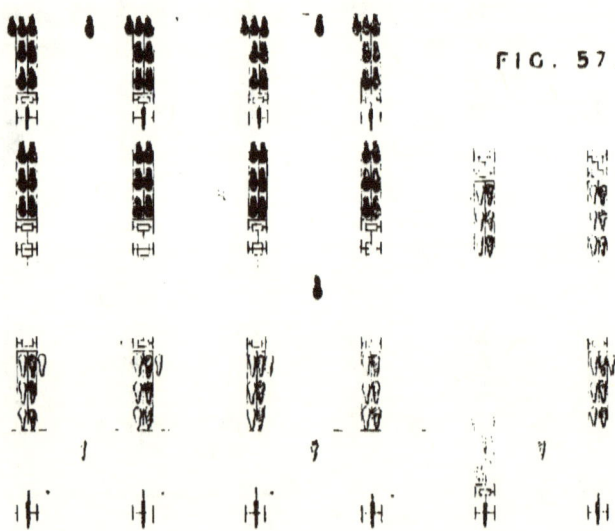

FIG. 57.

In Battery to form in Line to the Rear, with Pieces in Front.

Evans & Cogswell, Lith, Columbia, S.C.

Pl. 37

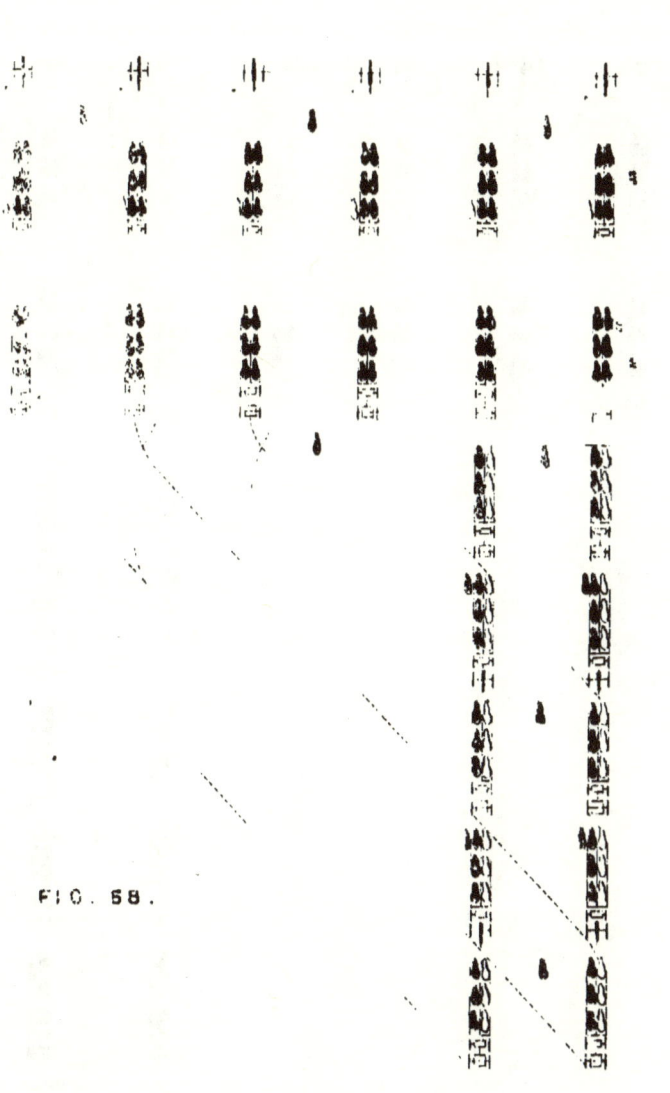

FIG. 58.

In Column, with Pieces in Front, to form in Battery to the Front.

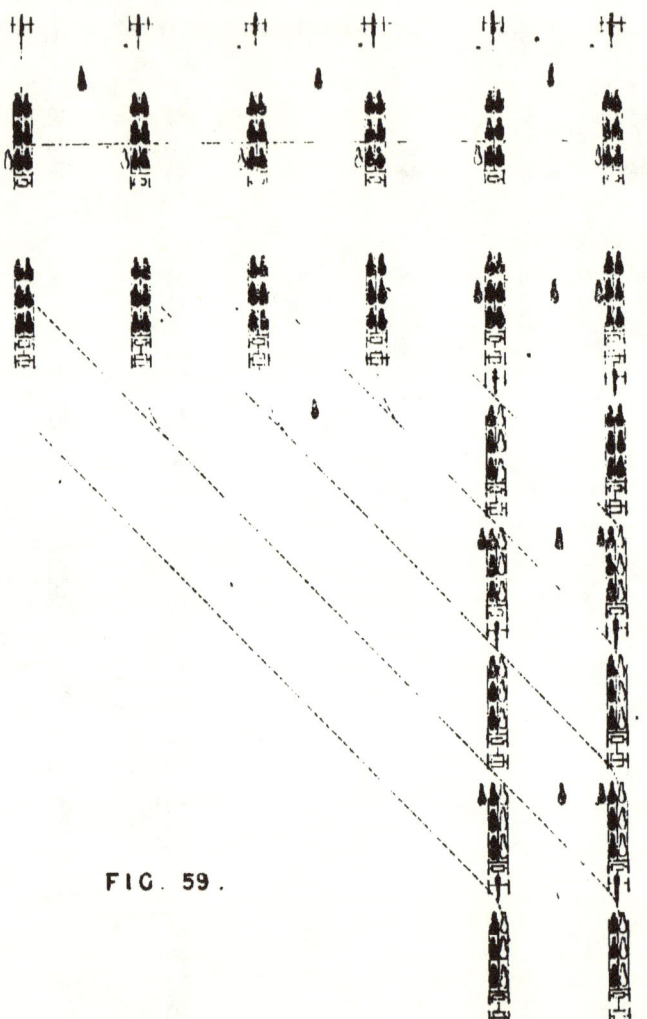

FIG. 59.

by Column, with Caissons in Front, to form in Battery to the Front

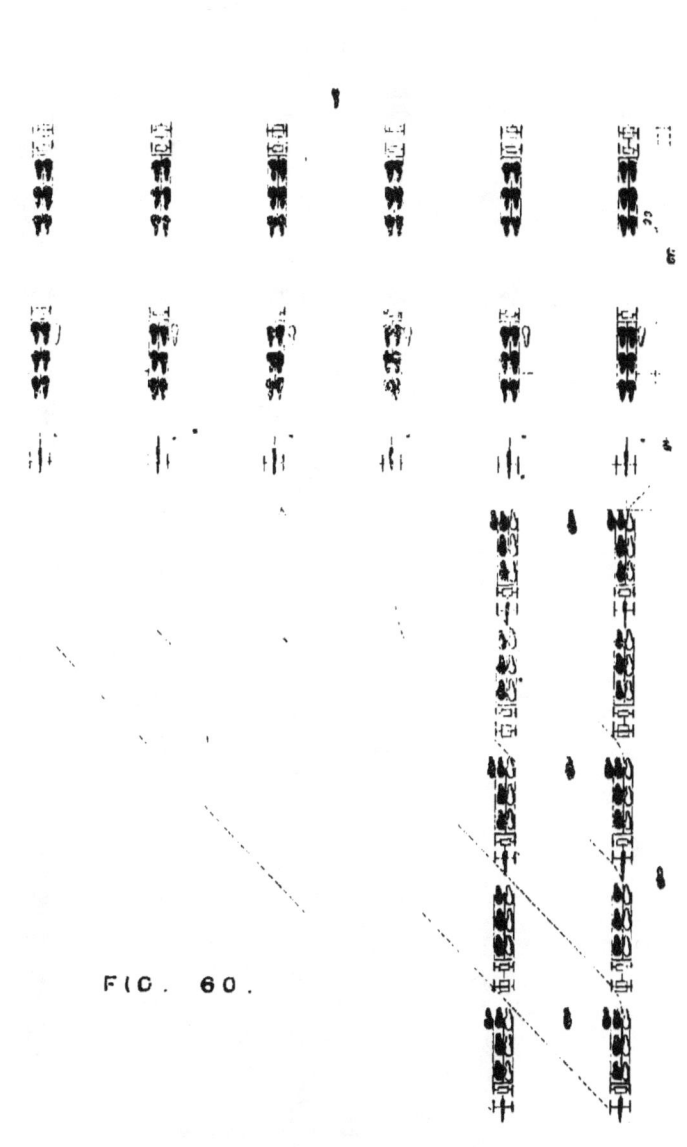

FIG. 60.

In Column with Pieces in front, to form in Battery to the Rear.

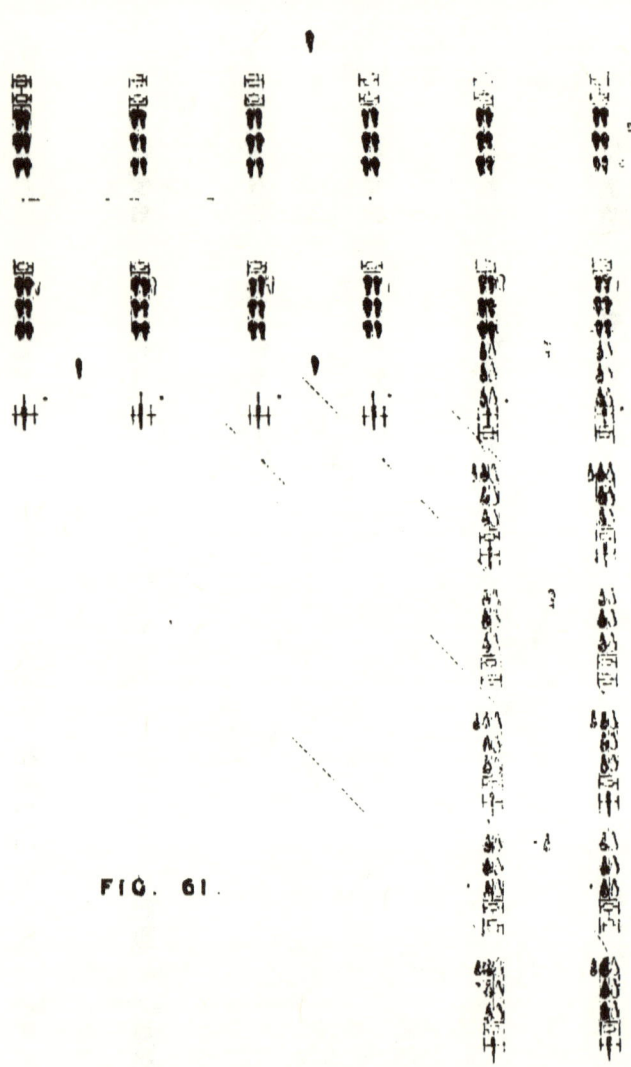

FIG. 61.

In Column, with Caissons in Front, to form in Battery to the Rear.

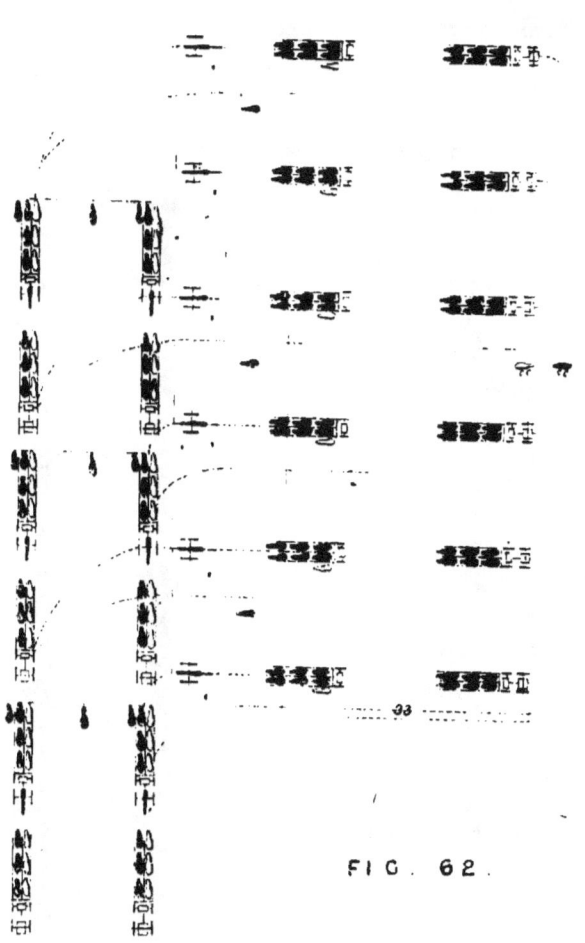

FIG. 62.

b. Column with pieces in Front, to form in Battery to the Left, gaining ground to the Right.

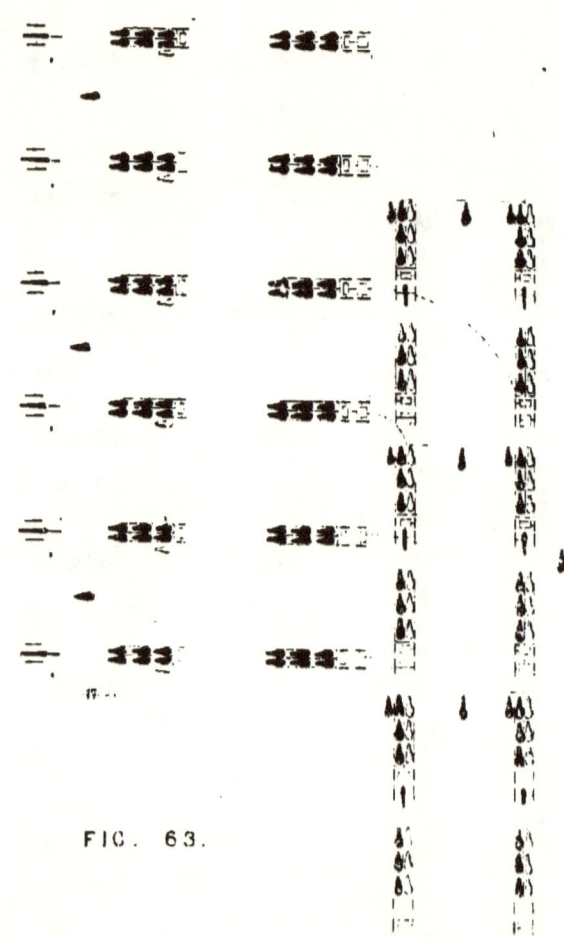

FIG. 63.

In Column, with Pieces in Front, to form in Battery to the Left, gaining ground to the left.

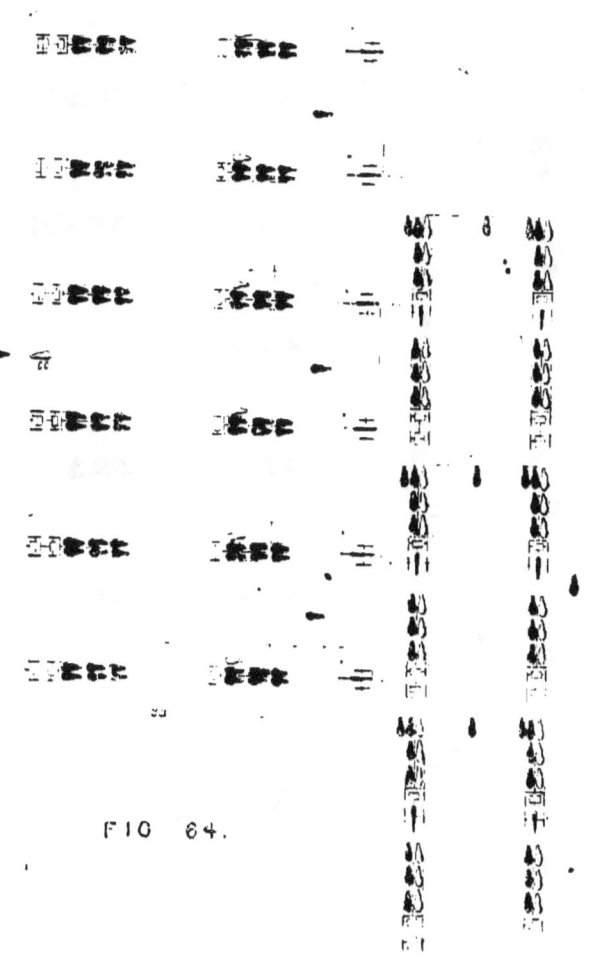

FIG 64.

In Column, with Pieces in Front, to form in Battery to the Right
gaining ground to the Left.

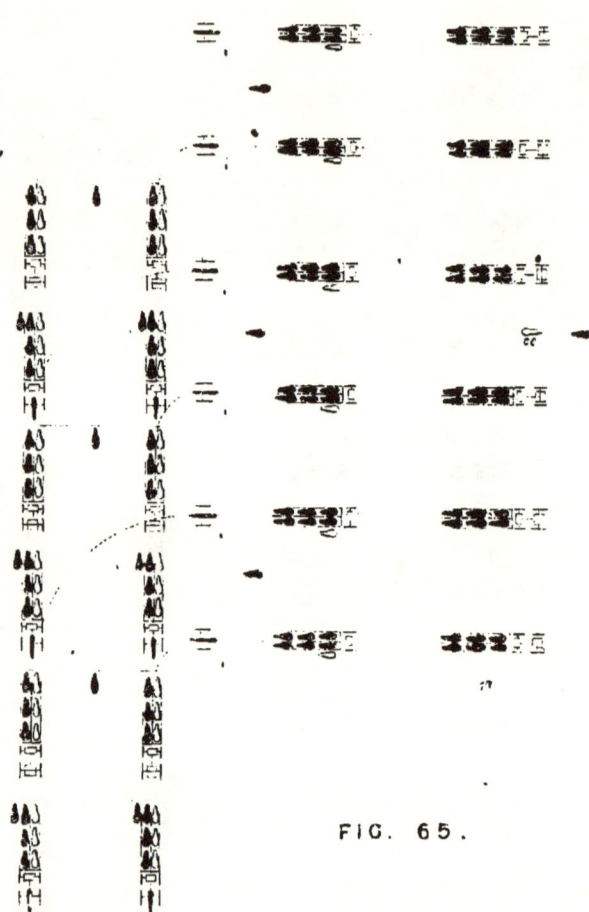

FIG. 65.

In Column, with Caissons in Front, to form in Battery to the Left, gaining ground to the Right.

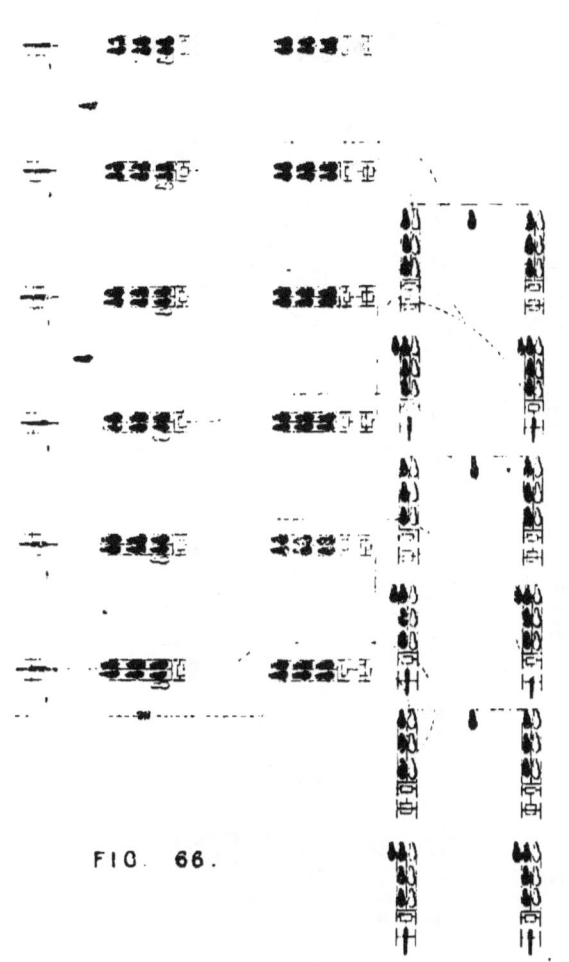

FIG. 66.

In Column, with Caissons in front to form in Battery to the Left, gaining ground to the Left.

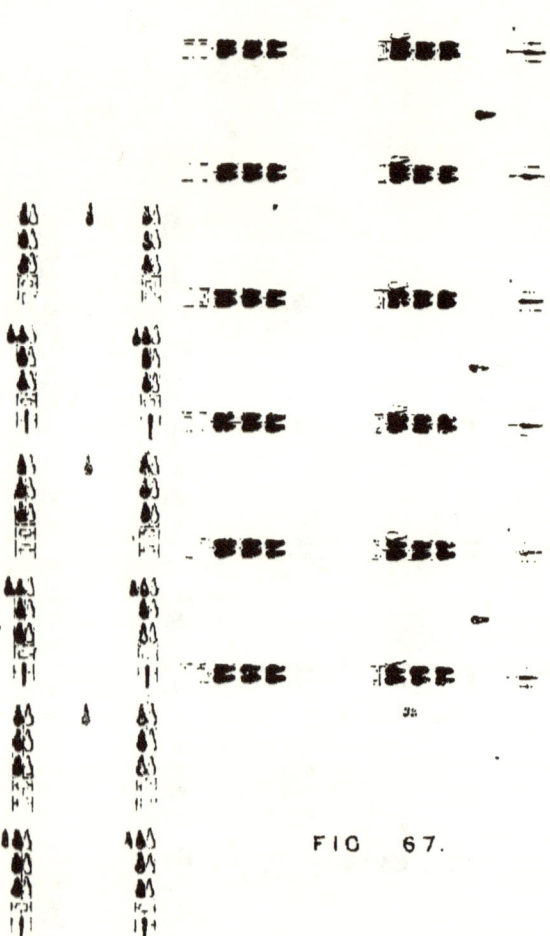

FIG 67.

In Column, with *guns* in Front, to form in Battery to the Right, gaining ground to the Right.

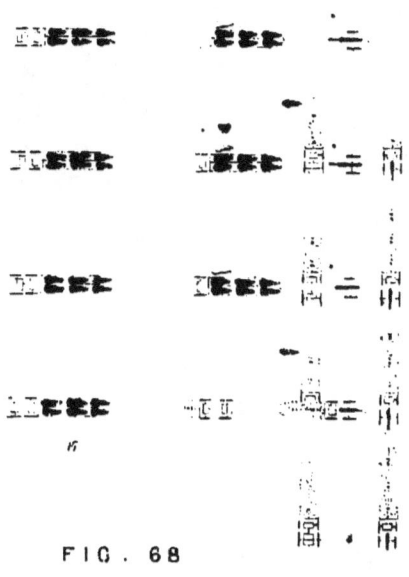

FIG. 68

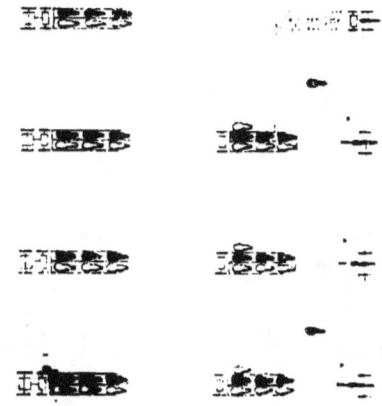

In Battery to March to the Left & form again in Battery

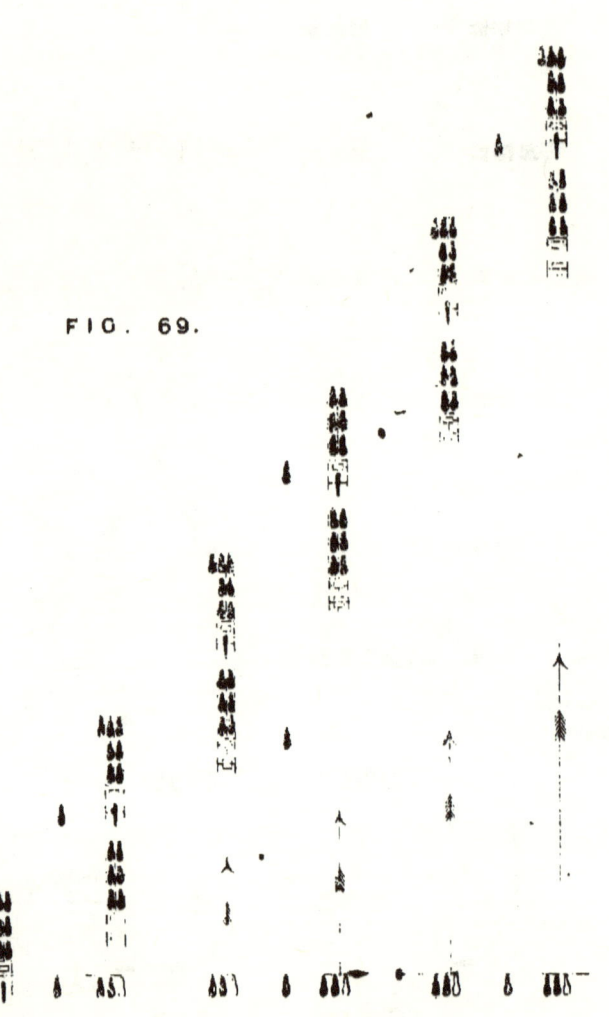

FIG. 69.

Echelon.

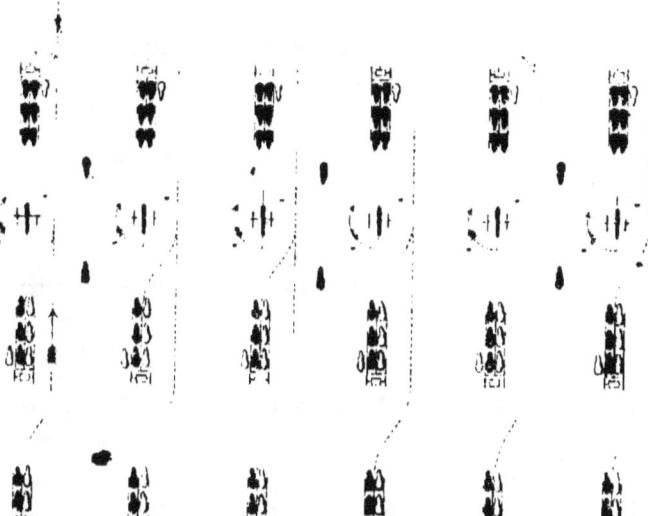

FIG. 70.

To Fire to the Rear.

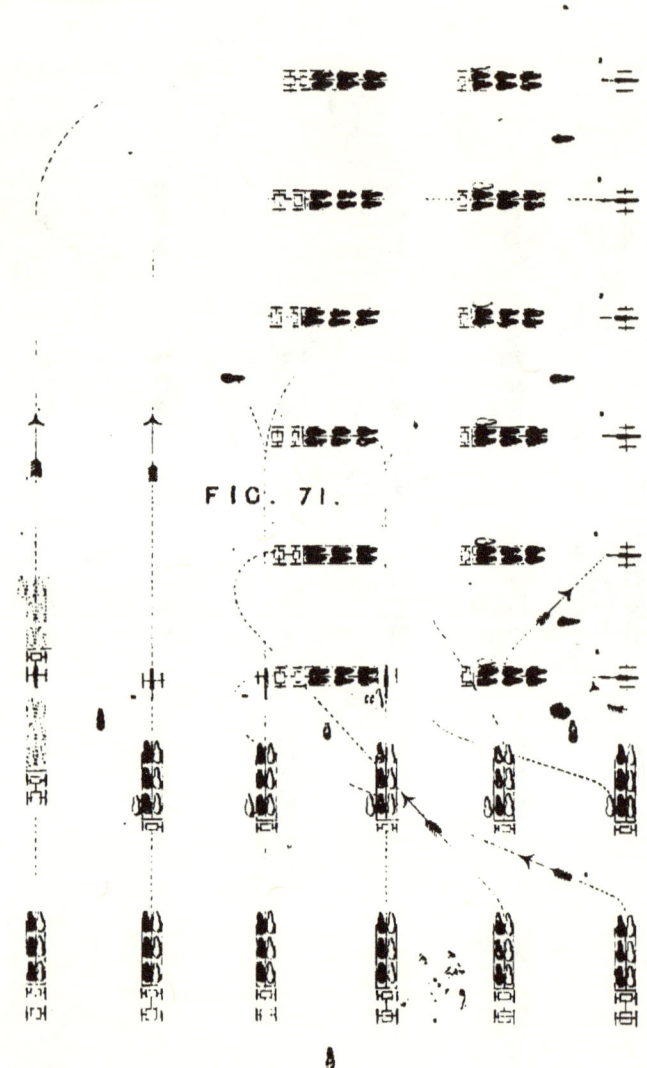

FIG. 71.

Fire to the Right. Change Front forward on First Piece

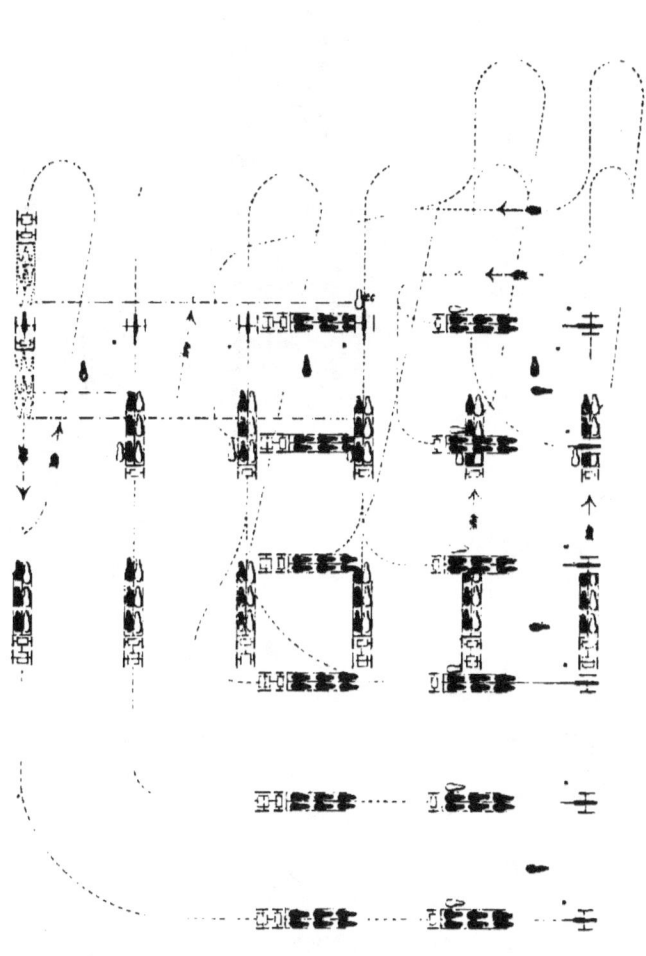

FIG. 72.

Fire to the Right — Change Front to Rear on Right Piece.

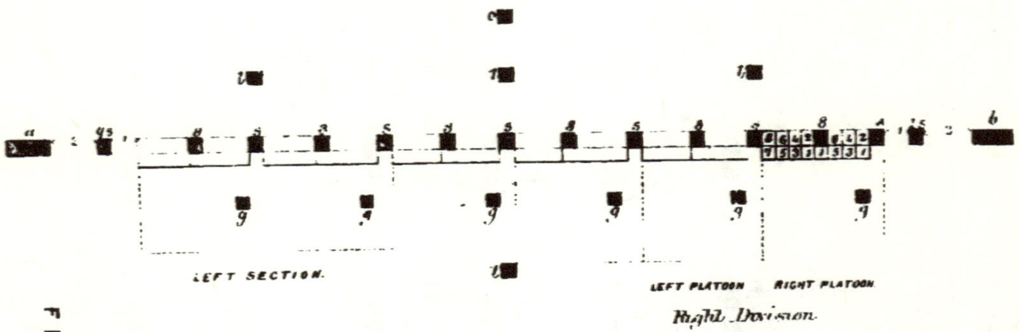

FIG. 73.

c. Captain.
l. Lieutenant.
1.s. First Sergeant.
q.s. Quartermaster Sergeant.
s. Sergeant.
g. Gunner.
8. N° 8. Detachment.
a. Artificers.
b. Buglers.

LEFT SECTION.
LEFT PLATOON. RIGHT PLATOON.
Right Division.

Order in Line, Dismounted.

Pl. 53

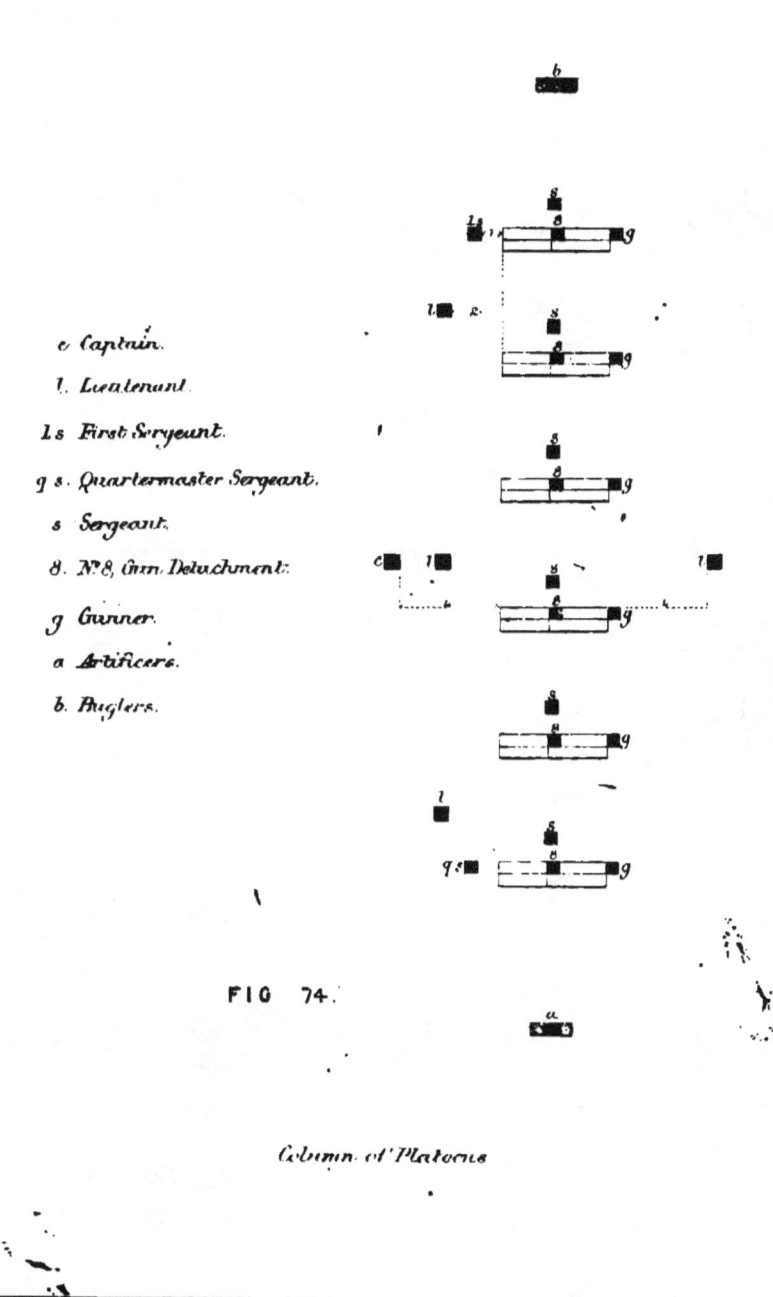

c. Captain.
l. Lieutenant.
1 s. First Sergeant.
q s. Quartermaster Sergeant.
s. Sergeant.
8. No. 8, Gun Detachment.
g. Gunner.
a. Artificers.
b. Buglers.

FIG 74.

Column of Platoons

13. DRIVERS MOUNT.

14. DRIVERS DISMOUNT.

15. CANNONEERS MOUNT.

16. IN BATTERY.

17. COMMENCE FIRING.

18. CEASE FIRING.

19. BOOTS & SADDLES.

www.ingramcontent.com/pod-product-compliance
Lightning Source LLC
Chambersburg PA
CBHW021832230426
43669CB00008B/942